ITIL® 4: Digital and IT Strategy (DITS)

Your companion to the ITIL® 4 Strategic Leader DITS certification

ITIL® 4: Digital and IT Strategy (DITS)

Your companion to the ITIL® 4 Strategic Leader DITS certification

CLAIRE AGUTTER

IT Governance Publishing

IT Governance Publishing Ltd
Unit 3, Clive Court
Bartholomew's Walk
Cambridgeshire Business Park
Ely, Cambridgeshire
CB7 4EA
United Kingdom
www.itgovernancepublishing.co.uk

First edition published in the United Kingdom in 2024 by IT Governance Publishing

ISBN 978-1-78778-426-0

ABOUT THE AUTHOR

Claire Agutter is a service management trainer, consultant and author. From 2018-23, she was nominated by Computer Weekly as one of the most influential women in tech. In 2018, 2019 and 2024, she was recognised as an HDI Top 25 Thought Leader and was part of the team that won itSMF UK's 2017 Thought Leadership Award. Claire is the chief architect for VeriSM™, the service management approach for the digital age. She is the director of Scopism, focusing on best practices for service integration and management (SIAM). Claire has worked with ITGP to publish *Service Integration and Management (SIAM™) Foundation Body of Knowledge (BoK), Second edition* and *Service Integration and Management (SIAM™) Professional Body of Knowledge (BoK), Second edition*, the official guides for the EXIN SIAM™ Foundation and Professional certifications.

After providing support to thousands of people taking ITIL training and certification from version 2 onwards, Claire has created this series of books for those studying towards ITIL® 4 Managing Professional and Strategic Leader status.

For more information, please visit:

- *www.scopism.com*

Contact:

- *www.linkedin.com/in/claireagutter/*
- *https://x.com/ClaireAgutter*

For more information about Claire's other publications with ITGP, visit:

www.itgovernancepublishing.co.uk/author/claire-agutter

ACKNOWLEDGEMENTS

This book is dedicated to Vicki England, for all of her support.

CONTENTS

INTRODUCTION

How to use this book

As you read the book, assume that all the content is related to the syllabus unless it is highlighted in one of two ways:

Something for you: a small exercise for you to complete to apply the ITIL® 4 concepts in your own role, or a point for you to think about. This content is not examinable.

Practical experiences: any content marked out with this image is based on my own experience and is not examinable.

The content highlighted as something for you to think about or practical experience might also refer to the Banksbest case study you can find in Appendix A. I'll use the case study to give an example of how something would work in the real world, or to help you apply what you're reading about. Case studies can really help to bring abstract concepts to life. The case study is not examinable but using it will help you get a deeper understanding of the ITIL® 4: Digital and IT Strategy concepts. Let's start with something for you now:

Why not read the case study and make a note of your first impressions of the Banksbest organisation and its plans before you start to study the ITIL® 4: Digital and IT Strategy content in this book? Is the strategy clear? Does it seem achievable?

CHAPTER 1: INTRODUCTION TO DIGITAL AND IT STRATEGY

In this chapter, we introduce Digital and IT Strategy and related key concepts. The topics in this chapter include:

- The target audience;
- Key learning outcomes;
- What's driving change?; and
- ITIL® 4: Digital and IT Strategy and the ITIL guiding principles.

The target audience

The target audience for the ITIL® 4: Digital and IT Strategy training and associated certification is a little different to some of the other ITIL training courses. The material is specifically aimed at:

- IT and business directors;
- Department heads;
- C-suite professionals;
- Leaders who are involved in digital change; and
- Consultants who are working with organisations that are digitally transforming.

So, if you're not in a senior role, does that mean this content isn't for you? Absolutely not! Perhaps you aspire to a more senior role in the future, in which case you'll gain valuable knowledge. And even if you don't aspire to a seat in the boardroom, an understanding of strategic concepts will absolutely help you perform any service management role.

Next time you find yourself thinking 'why on earth are the management team insisting on this?', you may have the answer from your new ability to link organisational decisions to strategic drivers.

In my experience, it can be really challenging to get senior people to attend training courses, particularly if there's an examination at the end. Senior people often have very little time in their calendars, so a generic training course that's not directly linked to their own organisation and its objectives may not seem to be worth the effort. Some years ago, I taught an ITIL® Foundation class to a group from an organisation, with roles from service desk analyst through to service manager on the course. On the first day, the CIO popped his head round the door. "I want you to listen to this stuff," he said. "It's important". And we never saw him again!

If you're trying to create change in your organisation and you're not in a senior role, you may need to explain important concepts to your potential sponsors to try to win their support. Focus on the value you want to deliver and the outcomes you're trying to achieve, NOT on the fact that you're 'doing ITIL'. That way, you'll be much more likely to succeed. Bear that in mind as you read the rest of this book – there is a lot of focus on outcomes and value, just as there should be.

ITIL® 4: Digital and IT Strategy outcomes

The material that you study as part of this training and certification will give you the tools to:

- Develop a cross-organisational digital strategy;
- Create a digital vision;
- Drive operational excellence;
- Respond effectively to digital disruption;
- Enable a sustainable business;
- Manage risk strategically; and
- Develop other digital leaders for the future.

Of course, as with any training, the real gains come from when and how you apply your knowledge. As you study, think about what opportunities you have in your current role to apply what you have learned.

It's important to remember that strategic planning is more art than science. The table below shows a summary of what ITIL® 4: Digital and IT Strategy is, and more importantly, what it isn't.

Table 1: What ITIL® 4: Digital and IT Strategy is, and what it isn't

ITIL® 4: Digital and IT Strategy is...	ITIL® 4: Digital and IT Strategy is not...
An examination of the role of strategy in a digitally enabled organisation	A 'how to' guide to creating a strategy for your organisation
An overview of the capabilities needed to compete in a digital world	A list of dos and don'ts

About how to evaluate new technology and its potential for competitive differentiation	An overview of specific emerging technologies and how to use them
A way of thinking about innovation so that organisations can prepare for the continual development of disruptive technology	A forecast of the next wave of ideas and technologies that will disrupt the industry

Think about some examples of how technology has disrupted industries. You might think about Uber and the taxi industry, or Airbnb and the hotel industry. You might have started to use artificial intelligence (AI) in your day-to-day work such as ChatGPT or Microsoft Copilot. Nearly every daily activity has been touched by technology, from making a payment to booking an appointment. For some industries, technology offers small, operational improvements. For others, it's a radical transformation.

There are ethical, moral and legal questions that need to be considered as part of our strategic planning. A friend who works in voiceover for films and animations said that there are companies that are taking short recordings of voiceover work and using AI to create a digital artist who can provide a very similar product for a fraction of the price. Legal? Yes, currently. Ethical? If the original artist isn't getting paid, probably not.

How an organisation responds to digital disruption has many facets. Not responding at all isn't a serious option.

What's driving change?

The concepts in the ITIL® 4: Digital and IT Strategy material are important because digital and information technology are changing the world. Business models are changing rapidly, putting pressure on business leaders, and the rate of innovation acceleration means that organisational change management has never been more critical.

Figure 1 shows the impact that digital advancements are having on every element of the organisation.[1]

[1] *ITIL® 4: Digital and IT Strategy*, Figure 1.2. ITIL® is a registered trade mark of the PeopleCert group. Used under licence from PeopleCert. All rights reserved.

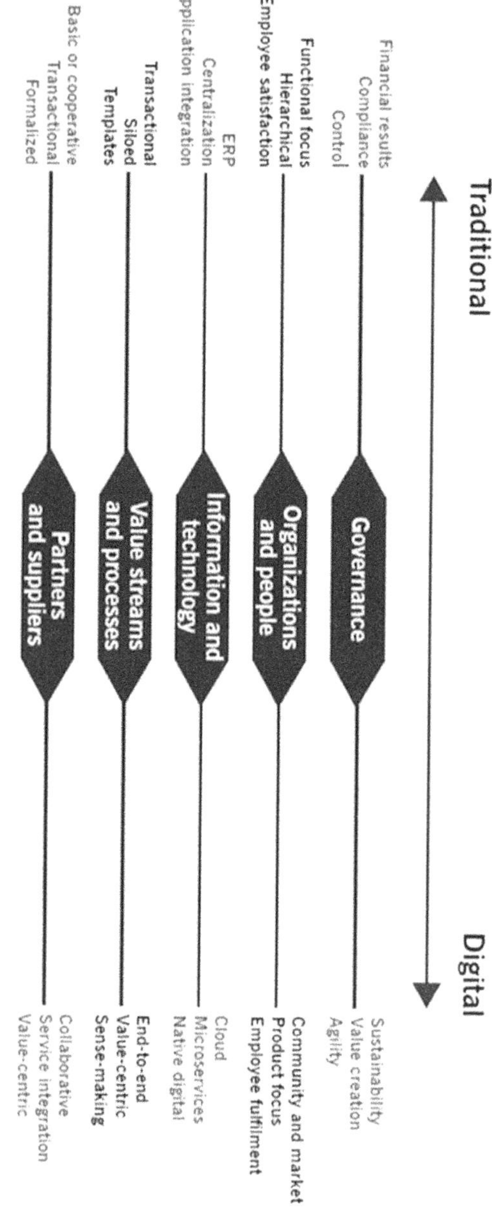

Figure 1: Governance and management shift from traditional to digital organizations

The pace of change has had an impact on the lifecycle of products and services, from development through to retirement. The figure below shows how the traditional innovation cycle (plan, build, run) has been replaced by a much more complex cycle that allows for iteration, experimentation and ongoing change.

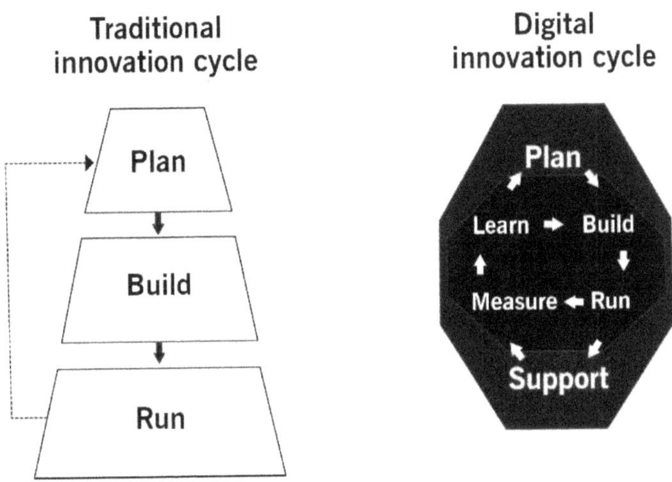

Figure 2: Traditional vs continual innovation cycle[2]

Technology can help organisations adapt to the acceleration of innovation.

[2] *ITIL® 4: Digital and IT Strategy*, Figure 1.3. ITIL® is a registered trade mark of the PeopleCert group. Used under licence from PeopleCert. All rights reserved.

One area where technology is having a real impact is the rise of the 'digital worker'. It's a broadly accepted fact that organisations won't invest in automation when human labour is cheaply available. As the price of human workers rises, organisations will invest in automation as the business case has changed. More and more countries now report a digital skills shortage, which is also driving the rise of the digital workforce.

But is this all bad? Are robots taking our jobs? Not necessarily.

In fact, the rise of digital workers means that many mundane, dull and repetitive tasks can now be carried out without human intervention. While this may mean some jobs disappear, it also means that human staff are freed up to do more interesting work that gives them satisfaction and delivers better value to their employer. A win-win.

Figure 3 shows what happens when innovation accelerates.[3]

[3] *ITIL® 4: Digital and IT Strategy*, Figure 1.4. ITIL® is a registered trade mark of the PeopleCert group. Used under licence from PeopleCert. All rights reserved.

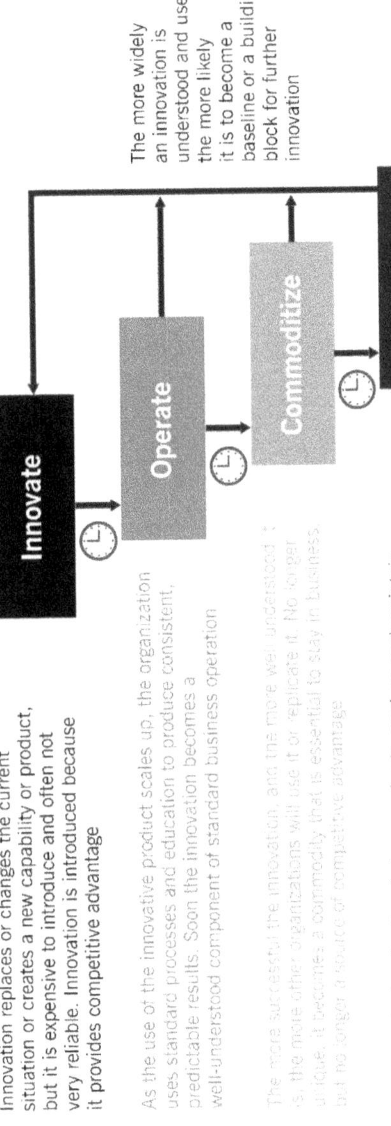

Figure 3: What happens when innovation accelerates

The big capability gap that I see with the organisations that I'm working with is between 'digital first' organisations that have always worked with digital technologies and 'legacy' (I don't love this phrase!) organisations that are having to adapt to the rise of technology.

Digital-first organisations may find it easier to adopt new ways of working and emerging technologies because they've always worked that way, whereas legacy organisations may have some cultural changes that need to take place. With these legacy organisations, I'm often asked to help them unite the old and the new ways of working; for example, 'How do I get my Agile teams to follow the change management process?'. Clashes between old and new schools of thinking need to be understood and friction points need to be removed. Not everything 'old' is bad!

ITIL® 4: Digital and IT Strategy and the ITIL guiding principles

As a reminder, the ITIL guiding principles are:

- Focus on value
- Start where you are
- Progress iteratively with feedback
- Collaborate and promote visibility
- Think and work holistically

- Keep it simple and practical
- Optimise and automate

From the ITIL® 4: Digital and IT Strategy perspective, we can apply the guiding principles to strategy development and strategic thinking. The guiding principles provide a start point or an example, and some organisations will have additional guiding principles that they apply for their own context and environment.

Having guiding principles that are clearly defined and shared at all levels of the organisation supports effective decision making. Whether a decision is required at the operational, tactical or strategic level, an organisation's guiding principles will help the person making it decide effectively.

Here's an exercise for you. After reading the Banksbest case study, can you think of any additional guiding principles that they might develop for their organisation?

You can also do some research online to try to find other organisations that share their guiding principles (Zappos is an example to start with). Do you know your own organisation's guiding principles? Or any organisation you have previously worked with?

Table 2 further explains the guiding principles.

Table 2: Description of seven guiding principles[4]

Guiding principle	***Description***
Focus on value	*"All of the organization's actions must translate, either directly or indirectly, into value for the stakeholders."*
Start where you are	*"Do not start from scratch and build something new, without considering what is already available."*
Progress iteratively with feedback	*"Do not attempt to do everything at once. Using feedback ensures that actions are focused and appropriate, even if circumstances change."*
Collaborate and promote visibility	*"Collaborating across boundaries produces results that have greater buy-in, relevance to objectives, and increased likelihood of long-term success."*
Think and work holistically	*"Outcomes achieved by the service provider and service consumer will suffer unless the organization works on the service in its entirety."*

[4] *ITIL® 4: Digital and IT Strategy*, Table 2.3. ITIL® is a registered trade mark of the PeopleCert group. Used under licence from PeopleCert.

Keep it simple and practical	*"Use the minimum number of steps necessary to accomplish the objective(s). Outcome-based thinking."*
Optimize and automate	*"Eliminate anything that is wasteful and use technology to its full capabilities."*

CHAPTER 2: KEY CONCEPTS

In this chapter, we'll study key concepts that support the creation and management of digital and IT strategies. This chapter includes:

- Digital technology;
- Digital business;
- Digital organisation;
- Digitisation;
- Transformation;
- Products and services and their management;
- Strategy tiers; and
- Business models.

Digital technology

Digital technology is "*any technology that digitizes something or processes digital data. Digital technology refers to information technology (IT) and the parts of operational technology (OT) that have been digitized. It also depends on the use of communications technology. Thus, digital technology refers to the merging of IT, OT and communications technology to achieve levels of functionality and automation that are not possible with any of these alone.*"

Figure 4 shows the hierarchy of elements within the digital technology definition.

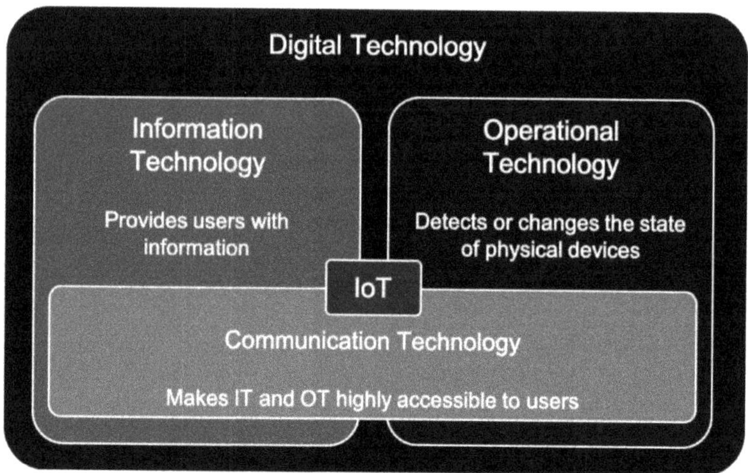

Figure 4: Digital technology[5]

The different elements of digital technology can be confusing. Let's take an example from the agricultural industry. Digital technology is now being applied to crop management, allowing farmers to look after their crops in a cost-efficient way that also helps the environment. Historically, farmers had to treat their entire crops with weedkillers, pesticides, watering, etc. Now, technology allows them to be much more targeted.

[5] *ITIL® 4: Digital and IT Strategy*, Figure 2.1. ITIL® is a registered trade mark of the PeopleCert group. Used under licence from PeopleCert. All rights reserved.

Drones (OT) can fly above fields to report on the status of a crop and signal where there are weeds or pest damage, or signs of drought using AI to compare images of healthy crops with those that are in danger. Information technology allows the farmer to review and assess images, and the corrective action (weedkiller, pesticide) can be applied either manually or in an automated way. Over time, the information will build so that trends can be seen, particular seed types reviewed, etc.

Table 3, below, provides further detail on the elements of digital technology.

Table 3: IT, OT, CT and IoT definitions

Term	Explanation
Information technology (IT)	Information technology refers to the use of systems to store, retrieve and send information. The systems may include software, hardware, services and infrastructure. Word processing or spreadsheets are examples of information technology.
Operational technology (OT)	Operational technology refers to systems or devices that monitor and/or control devices, processes and events. Examples of operational technology include fire control systems or cyber security threat monitoring. OT can form part of the Internet of things (IoT).

Communication technology (CT)	ITIL® 4 defines communication technology as *"...enables IT and OT to be highly mobile and accessible to organizations, consumers and other stakeholders"*. Common examples of communication technology are email, video conferencing and online chat.
Internet of things (IoT)	The Internet of things (IoT) describes a network of devices that are connected to the Internet and can send and receive data. Do you want your fridge to automatically order milk when you're getting low? You need a smart fridge with IoT capabilities!

Digital business

In the ITIL® 4 definition, digital business describes how organisations use digital technology to carry out activities. The definition of digital business relates to 'carrying out business' rather than 'a business' as an entity.

Here's something for you to think about. For your current or most recent employer, what activities are now enabled by technology that weren't in the past? Is technology part of their core strategy, or more related to operational efficiencies?

One of the businesses that I started is an elearning organisation. From day one (16 years ago), we've only done elearning and we could only exist because of technology. We could perhaps have offered classroom training instead, but that would have put us in a very different competitive environment; local customers instead of global, for example.

Digital organisation

"A digital organization is an organization that is enabled by digital technology to do business significantly differently, or to do a significantly different business."

Most organisations operate using a mixture of systems, including both digital and manual activities. Digital organisations are very reliant on technology to carry out their core business activities (do 'digital business').

There's a trend at the moment to put 'digital' in front of everything – digital business, digital worker, digital leaders, digital teams, etc. It can be helpful or it can cloud what we're trying to say, so it's important to assess the word as we use it. Digital business is, I believe, an important definition because it describes a significant change in how organisations operate and how they view themselves. It describes a way of thinking that moves from 'IT and the business' to 'IT is the business'.

We need to apply 'digital' with care though and not lose sight of our customers or the outcomes we want to achieve. An example here comes from the UK's health service and the rollout of the COVID-19 pass that allowed people to travel by showing their vaccination record and any COVID-19 infections/recoveries. Many people thought of this as a 'digital' service hosted in an app, but in fact it needed both an online and offline element, for people who didn't use the Internet or weren't comfortable using an app. The outcome and the value came from being able to record and share information about people's COVID-19 history and vaccinations. The app/digital element was the major part of this, but it wasn't the whole story.

Digitisation

Digitisation turns something from analogue to digital. For example, a newspaper might decide to digitise its archive of previous editions. Digitisation can also refer to how we use digital technology to change an aspect of how we work – for example, "we digitised the new starter process".

Banksbest is digitising cheques. The new service My Deposit My Way will allow cheques to be paid in to bank accounts using the camera on a mobile phone. What are the benefits associated with this? Can you think of any risks?

Digital transformation

ITIL 4® defines digital transformation as *"the use of digital technology to enable a significant improvement in the realization of the organization's objectives that could not feasibly have been achieved by non-digital means. Digital transformation is achieved by digitizing, robotizing, and other forms of automation that enable organizations to do things differently, or to do different things."*

Figure 5 shows how digital transformation impacts all areas of the organisation. Viewing digital technology as an 'IT initiative' invites failure. This needs to be seen as a holistic, business-wide initiative, and integrated into day-to-day business activities.[6]

[6] *ITIL® 4: Digital and IT Strategy*, Figure 2.2. ITIL® is a registered trade mark of the PeopleCert group. Used under licence from PeopleCert. All rights reserved.

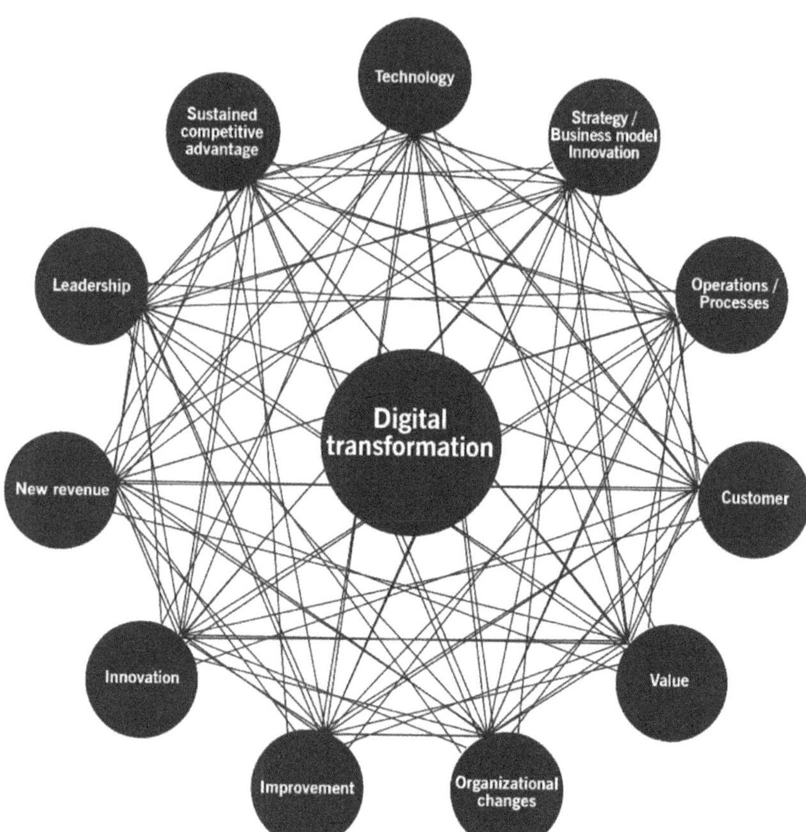

Figure 5: Modified list of key digital transformation themes

Products and services and their management

Most organisations create products and services to help them fulfil their strategic objectives. Products and services are often the point where organisations interact with their consumers, and where value is co-created.

Banksbest has set itself a strategic target to grow its residential mortgage business by 50%. What actions could it take to help realise this goal? How many of them are technology related or supported by technology?

The terms in the table below will be familiar to you from your ITIL® 4 Foundation training. They are the ingredients that an organisation has to work with to serve its consumers. And just like with recipes, the ingredients can be combined in different ways to deliver very different outcomes.

Table 4: Resource, product, service and service offering definitions

Term	Definition
Resource	*"A person or other entity that is required for executing an activity or achieving an objective."*
Product	*"A configuration of an organization's resources, designed to offer value for a consumer."*
Service	*"A means of enabling value co-creation by facilitating outcomes that customers want to achieve, without the customer having to manage specific costs and risks."*

Service offering	*"Describes one or more services based on one or more products. Service offerings might include goods, access to resources, and service actions."*

Creating competitive advantage/Wardley mapping

Wardley mapping[7] is a technique that can help organisations understand their products and services and how they can add to (or detract from) an organisation's level of competitiveness. Wardley maps support strategic decision-making and provide a way to have conversations about the organisation's products and services. The maps are based on the five factors from Sun Tzu's *The Art of War*:

- **Purpose:** the scope of what is being done and why.
- **Landscape:** the (competitive) environment.
- **Climate:** what forces are acting on the organisation's leaders.
- **Doctrine:** principles (in this case, the ITIL® 4 guiding principles are a good place to start).
- **Leadership:** context-specific decisions and strategy taking all factors into account.

The five factors can be combined with the OODA loop (observe, orient, decide, act), as shown in Figure 6[8]:

---

[7] For more information on Wardley maps, visit https://medium.com/wardleymaps.

[8] *ITIL® 4: Digital and IT Strategy*, Figure 2.3. ITIL® is a registered trade mark of the PeopleCert group. Used under licence from PeopleCert. All rights reserved.

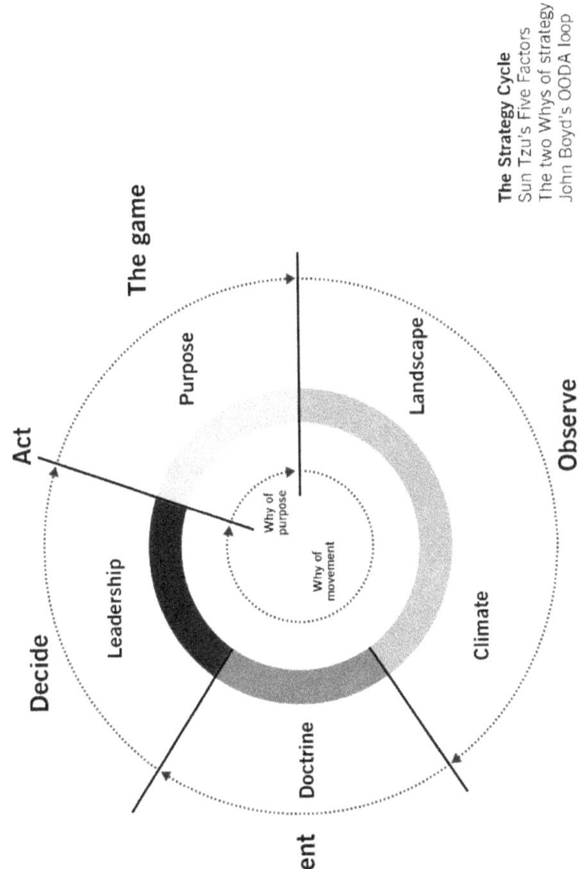

Figure 6: Wardley's strategy cycle
Reproduced under creative commons from Wardley (2017)

Situational awareness

The outputs from the strategy cycle and Wardley mapping can be used to define or confirm a proposed action, or series of actions. Strategic planning is important, but should ultimately lead to action – if not, the organisation is paralysed. Once an organisation understands its situation (situational awareness), decisions can be made, leading ultimately to action being taken. Figure 7 shows this flow[9]:

[9] *ITIL® 4: Digital and IT Strategy*, Figure 2.4. Cited from Wardley, S. (2016) Wardley maps: topographical intelligence in business, *https://medium.com/wardleymaps*. ITIL® is a registered trade mark of the PeopleCert group. Used under licence from PeopleCert. All rights reserved.

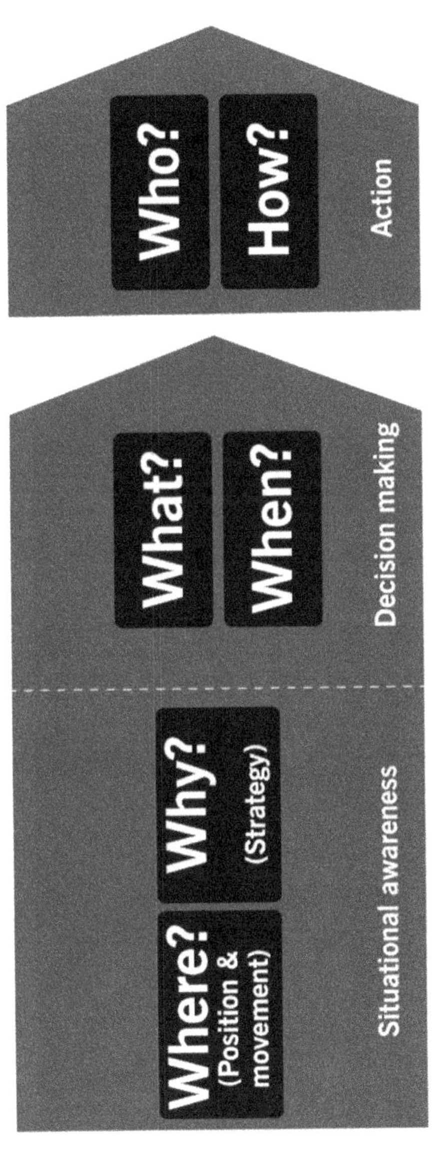

Figure 7: Situational awareness vs action

When the decisions that are made introduce new elements to the organisation (for example, products, services or ways of working), there will be an impact on existing products, services and business processes. Any change that is made should not happen in isolation; the organisational change needs to be managed to prevent any negative effect.

We just learned about how *"when the decisions that are made introduce new elements to the organisation (for example, products, services or ways of working), there will be an impact on existing products, services and business processes"*. This should be true, but one area I've seen this done very poorly is in organisations that grow through mergers and acquisitions.

The idea behind a merger or an acquisition is that the two organisations will come together and become something that is greater than the sum of its parts. If the acquired organisation, for example, has excellent technical capabilities, these will be shared with the acquiring organisation. What seems to happen instead is that the acquired organisation continues as a silo within the acquiring organisation and the benefits aren't shared.

The same effect can also be seen when a team in an organisation adopts a new way of working that is effective but only in its silo. It's a good idea to continually review your organisation and look for any local improvements that can be adopted more widely.

Strategy tiers

In many organisations, high-level goals are set and strategic planning takes place at the very top levels of management. The strategy is then shared with the rest of the organisation, cascading down into departments, into teams and to individuals to allow them to make their own plans that align with the overall strategy. This creates a 'tiered' structure, with the business strategy at the top and other strategies such as the IT or digital strategy then being created lower down in the organisation.

Do you know your own organisational strategy? For your employer, or a previous employer?

If you don't know it, how could you find out more? What would it mean when you had to make a difficult decision without this important context?

The increased importance of digital products and services and their integration with business processes requires a different perspective. Figure 8 shows an alternative to a traditional tiered approach.

Figure 8: Revised perspective (example) of business, digital, and IT strategy[10]

We need to consider the terms from this figure in more detail to support your ITIL® 4: Digital and IT Strategy studies.

[10] *ITIL® 4: Digital and IT Strategy*, Figure 2.6. ITIL® is a registered trade mark of the PeopleCert group. Used under licence from PeopleCert. All rights reserved.

Business strategy

The business strategy outlines how an organisation *"defines and achieves its purpose"*. The strategy will typically include:

- How the vision and objectives will be defined, communicated and refined;
- The business model;
- How the organisation will align all the elements involved in delivery (think about the four dimensions of service management);
- Organisational guiding principles;
- Strategic plans (what is the course of action and how will resources be allocated?); and
- What the organisation will NOT do.

Note that to create a business strategy, an organisation must understand its purpose. What does it exist to do? Also, a strategy on paper is of limited value. The value from the strategic planning comes when it is clearly communicated and adopted by the organisation, at all levels.

Digital strategy

ITIL® 4 defines the digital strategy as *"a business strategy that is based all or in part on using digital technology to achieve its goals and purpose"*.

This is a business strategy that embraces emerging technology. It isn't a technical document that specifies what technology will be introduced; rather, it looks at areas where technology can enable new products and services or facilitate improvements to existing products and services.

The creation of a digital strategy implies recognition of how essential technology has become to business operations. Historically, many organisations have managed IT in a silo, or created digital teams that operate separately from the rest of the organisation. A digital strategy shows the organisation helps the whole organisation to understand:

- That technology is changing and it's changing the operating environment;
- If a response is necessary or if current operations are sufficient;
- Any identified opportunities available within the digital landscape;
- The risks associated with each opportunity; and
- How to create a plan that exploits the opportunities and mitigates risks.

Banksbest is adopting a digital strategy, and has three strategic goals defined in the case study. Are all the goals enabled by technology? What are the possible benefits and risks associated with the bank's new digital strategy? Are there any areas of emerging technology that you would recommend to them if you were engaged there?

IT strategy

An IT strategy may be:

- A component of the digital strategy;
- A technical/architectural document that supports the digital strategy; or
- A back-office/administrative document that supports the management of the IT estate (arguably, not a strategy, more of a management plan).

The IT strategy should allow an organisation to understand:

- How IT supports the business goals;
- Which technology underpins current and future business operations;
- How to use technology to support the digital strategy;
- How to adopt new technology as required; and
- The supply network that provides technology to the organisation.

Business model

A business model is a *"formal description of how an organization should be configured to provide value to customers based on its strategy"*.

A business model is a framework, typically including three major themes:

- Value realisation: how an organisation works to create value through services, products and offerings.
- How value is created, including relationships, channels, customer segments and revenue streams.
- How the organisation will fulfil its commitments and meet expectations.

A business model must be based on a viable financial model to allow the costs associated with the framework to be understood.

Business models should be easy to understand and can be a valuable tool to help support conversations at all levels of an organisation about both the current and future state. One way to visualise a business model is to use a business model canvas, shown in the figure below.

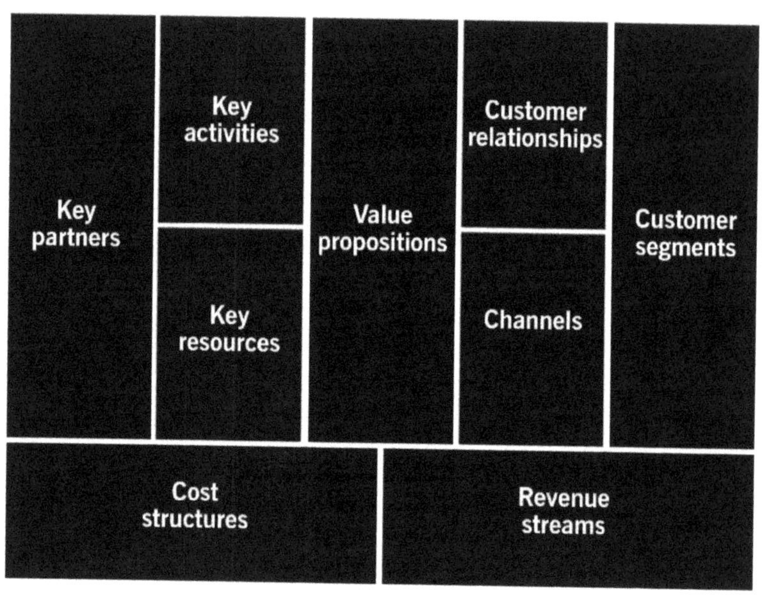

Figure 9: Business model canvas[11]

[11] *ITIL® 4: Digital and IT Strategy*, Figure 2.7. From Osterwalder, A. and Pigneur, Y. (2010). Business Model Generation: A Handbook for Visionaries, Game Changers, and Challengers. Wiley. ITIL® is a registered trade mark of the PeopleCert group. Used under licence from PeopleCert. All rights reserved.

The business model canvas shows how an organisation delivers value to its customers in a simple, easy-to-consume way. When an organisation has to make strategic decisions, a range of business model canvases can be prepared to support discussion and effective decision-making and illustrate the different options. An organisation might also create a business model canvas based on how its competitors operate, to identify any opportunities to improve its own operations.

Use the business model canvas shown in Figure 9 and complete it for Banksbest based on the information in the case study and any assumptions you need to make. You can also try this for your current or a previous employer. Does the completed canvas highlight any strategic areas that may need addressing? Perhaps a risk, or an unexploited opportunity?

Figure 10 shows a simple business model design template.[12]

[12] *ITIL® 4: Digital and IT Strategy*, Figure 2.8. From Boudreau, K. (2018), Notes on designing your company: creating, delivering, and capturing value. Havard Business School Strategy Unit Working Paper No. 16-131. *https://papers.ssrn.com/sol3/papers.cfm?abstract_id=2784718*. ITIL® is a registered trade mark of the PeopleCert group. Used under licence from PeopleCert. All rights reserved.

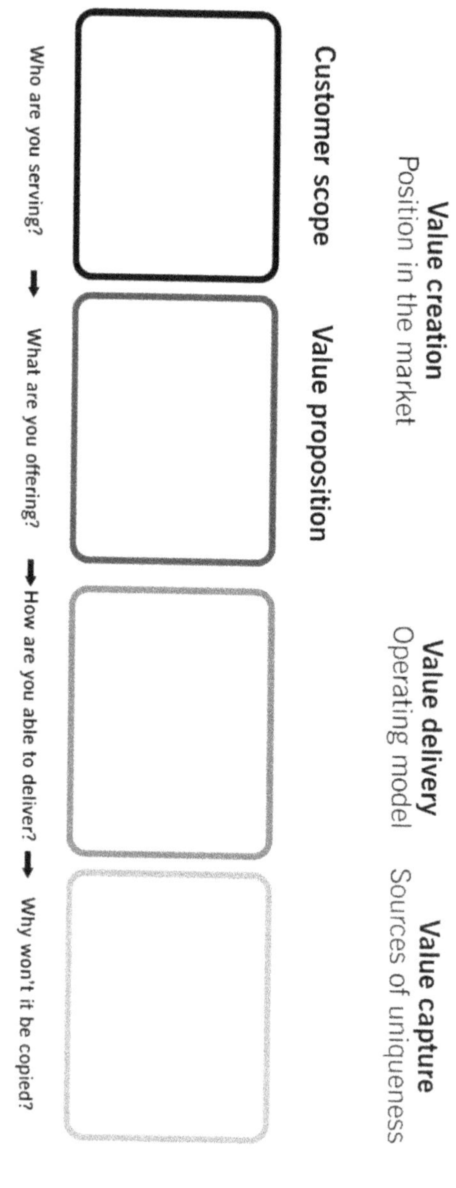

Figure 10: Adapted company design template

CHAPTER 3: DIGITAL AND IT STRATEGY AND THE SERVICE VALUE SYSTEM

In this chapter, we'll study the relationship between Digital and IT Strategy and the service value system (SVS). This chapter includes:

- Opportunity and demand;
- Value;
- Governance;
- Continual improvement;
- Practices;
- Practice: strategy management; and
- Environmental analysis.

Strategic planning should be based on the opportunities and demand that an organisation sees in its environment. The SVS and the service value chain express the organisation's strategy and provide a structure for plans and actions. The SVS describes how all the elements of an organisation interact to support value creation.

Opportunity and demand

An opportunity is *"a situation that allows an organization to expand its existing operation, either by introducing new products and services, or by moving into a new market"*.

Demand is *"an input to the SVS based on opportunities and needs of internal and external stakeholders"*. Demand can come from consumers of existing products and services, from new markets for existing products and services, and from new or existing markets for new products and services.

The strategy should define how the organisation responds to changes in demand.

There's a famous quote attributed to Henry Ford when asked about developing the car: *"If I had asked people what they wanted, they would have said faster horses."* There's not a lot of evidence that he said it, but there's a truth in there that we need to examine. Customers, consumers and users don't always know exactly what they want, and they don't always express their wants clearly.

A family member of mine left his job in IT to run a martial arts gym. He offered mixed classes, and a group of women who came to the class asked him to put on a women-only class in the evening. There were enough of them, and the desire was expressed strongly enough for him to create the women-only class. The first week, it was full. The second week, three people came. The week after, one person. Eventually, the class was removed from the rota.

What can we learn from this? First, demand isn't always clear. With digital services in particular, sometimes we have to show our consumers what is possible for them to fully understand how technology can transform what they do. Second, if we start small then the impact is reduced if we get things wrong. The cost for my family member was some extra room rental and some promotion. When the class was cancelled, the impact on the gym overall was minimal.

When an organisation experiences reducing demand for its products and services, it may choose to retire or replace them. It can also diversify into new areas, allowing the existing products and services to remain in place for current customers only until they reach a natural end of life.

Value

You will recall from your ITIL® 4 Foundation training that value is the *"perceived benefits, usefulness and importance of something"*. Value is co-created by the service provider and its consumers when the products and services are used.

Once a strategy is defined, tactical and operational planning will focus on the value associated with each product, service or value stream. Products and services should be described in terms of the outcomes they enable, for example reduced risk or increased efficiency. These benefits can be described in a unique value proposition (UVP), which helps the organisation encapsulate its vision in a short statement.

You can use Banksbest for this activity, or your own organisation. What is the unique value proposition for your chosen organisation? Create a short statement to encapsulate the vision based on the UVP.

Governance

Organisational governance is the *"system by which an organization is directed and controlled"*. The three major governance activities are as follows:

- **Evaluate** – the governing body evaluates strategy, the portfolio, etc., keeping in mind the stakeholder and their evolving needs.
- **Direct** – the governing body assigns responsibility for the preparation and implementation of the strategy and policies.
- **Monitor** – the governing body ensures performance conforms with policies and direction.

Governance should ensure that all of an organisation's strategies, policies, practices and decisions are aligned with its overall purpose.

Continual improvement

Continual improvement should take place at all levels of an organisation. It can be applied to an organisation's strategy in two ways:

- Via improvements to the strategy management practice, including activities and outputs.
- Via improvements to the organisation that can support the delivery of strategic goals.

Practices

A practice is a *"set of organizational resources designed for performing work or accomplishing an objective"*. A strategy will specify how an organisation will meet its objectives. The organisation's practices then provide the necessary processes, resources, partners, technology, etc.

The strategy management, portfolio management and architecture management practices map how organisational capabilities and assets support the organisation's desired outcomes. Practices need to evolve along with the organisation's strategy.

Practice: Strategy management

The purpose of the strategy management practice is to *"formulate the goals of the organization and adopt the courses of action and allocation of resources necessary for achieving those goals"*.

This isn't a one-off activity. The practice needs to be dynamic and purposeful to meet the needs of both internal and external stakeholders. The practice will be more effective if it combines data with insights, and is ultimately the responsibility of the organisation's executive leadership.

Strategy management will include long-, medium- and short-term elements. The vision, objectives and direction of the organisation will evolve over time, and strategy execution should be continually evaluated so it can be improved.

The strategy management practice works to ensure overall strategic alignment across other practices. It provides inputs to:

- Architecture management;
- Workforce and talent management;
- Risk management;
- Service financial management;
- Project management;

- Organisational change management;
- Portfolio management; and
- Relationship management.

Practice success factors

A practice success factor (PSF) is a *"complex functional component of a practice that is required for the practice to fulfil its purpose"*.

There are two PSFs defined for the strategy management practice:

- *"Ensuring that the organization's strategies are effective and sustainable, and meet the stakeholders' evolving needs*
- *Ensuring that the agreed strategies and models are communicated across the organization and embedded into the organization[']s practices and value streams"*

The table below describes the PSFs in more detail:

Table 5: Strategy management practice success factors

PSF: Ensuring strategies are effective and sustainable
Effective strategies match purpose, needs and requirements to the organisational vision, objectives, business and operating models. An effective strategy can be used to reinvent and stimulate conversation, to engage the entire organisation, and to support monitoring and execution of strategic activities. Strategic reports will be used to assess a strategy's effectiveness, including operational data and analysis of trends. Organisations may use techniques such as 'ALOE' (ask, listen, observe,

empathise) to support their assessment of strategic effectiveness. Organisations need to work to continually improve their emotional, social and system intelligence.

PSF: Strategies are communicated and embedded

A strategy must be embedded in the organisation and actively used to be effective. This can be supported by good communication, effective organisational change management, and a culture of continual improvement with the vision and principles embedded in it. All practices should be designed for strategic alignment and continual improvement.

The communication principles outlined in ITIL® 4: Direct, Plan and Improve support strategy communication:

- Communication is a two-way process.
- Communication happens continually.
- Communication timing and frequency are important.
- There is no 'one size fits all' method of communication.
- The medium affects the message.

Environment analysis

An organisation doesn't exist in isolation. Many external factors affect it, from the country it operates in and local legislation and regulation, to industry trends, to the needs of its customers and potential customers. Careful analysis of the environment will help an organisation develop an appropriate, effective strategy. In this section, we'll look at:

- External environment analysis;

- Internal environment analysis; and
- The interaction between the internal and the external.

External analysis

External analysis helps an organisation to understand:

- What needs exist in its environment;
- How important those needs are to consumers (which can include individuals or other organisations);
- How needs can be fulfilled using products and services;
- How needs change over time;
- What other organisations are already meeting those needs, and how effective they are; and
- The limitations of the environment and any constraints it imposes.

There are many techniques that can be used to assess the external environment. We'll look at some examples here, and you can always do more research if this area is relevant to you.

First, PESTLE (also sometimes shown as PESTEL) is a framework that can be used to analyse the environmental factors that can impact an organisation. It is used to monitor the external environment so that an organisation can remain relevant and adjust its strategy if needed.

Table 6 provides more detail about PESTLE.

Table 6: PESTLE

Factor	Description
Political	This includes the influence of government – tax, regulation, corruption, subsidies, protectionism, etc. For example, some countries have legislation that affects where data can be transferred to and processed.
Economic	Economic factors include inflation, interest rates, investment, etc. For example, high inflation may raise staffing costs in one geography, affecting the profitability of a service.
Social	Social factors include culture, values, demographics, etc. For example, social attitudes might make it hard to attract staff for organisations in certain sectors (e.g. tobacco, nuclear).
Technological	These factors relate to technology innovation, including incentives to automate, support for research and development, etc. For example, organisations may be able to reduce their tax liability by investing in research and development.
Legal	Legal factors relate specifically to legislation such as competition, employment, health and safety,

	environmental, etc. For example, legislation related to hardware disposal might increase service costs by forcing the use of registered hardware disposal organisations.
Environmental	These factors relate to geography, climate, pollution, natural resources, etc. For example, extreme weather events like flooding or heatwaves might need to be taken into consideration during service design.

Other possible techniques for external analysis include Porter's Five Forces and SWOT analysis. Porter's Five Forces is a framework for evaluating competition, new entrants, the power of suppliers, the power of customers and the threat of substitute products. Organisations can use Porter to assess their own value proposition and how to protect themselves from competitive threats.

SWOT analysis looks at the strengths, weaknesses, opportunities and threats that face an organisation. Opportunities and threats are usually external factors, and strengths and weaknesses are internal factors.

You may have used SWOT analysis in your career already. If you're not familiar with it, there are many examples available online. Practise a SWOT analysis now – you can use Banksbest or your own current or a previous employer. If you use Banksbest, you may need to make some assumptions to complete all the quadrants of the SWOT.

Internal analysis

Once the external analysis is complete, an organisation can look inward and assess what capabilities it has that will help it to succeed. Does it have the capabilities it needs now and in the future? What gaps exist? How can it improve?

The ITIL® 4 four dimensions of service management (organizations and people, information and technology, partners and suppliers, value streams and processes) provide a framework for assessing internal capabilities.

Table 7 shows some possible considerations for each of the four dimensions of service management.

Table 7: The four dimensions of service management and strategic planning

Dimension	Considerations
Organizations and people	Analysis here could include: • Structure/organisation chart; • Staff turnover/skills; • Culture; • Roles and responsibilities; and • Levels of empowerment and collaboration.
Information and technology	Analysis here could include: • Existing systems, data and level of exploitation; • Automation and use of 'digital workers'; and • Historical successes and failures with technical implementation.
Partners and suppliers	Analysis here could include: • Any legislative constraints; • Availability of partners with appropriate skills; • Costs; and • Internal supplier management capabilities.
Value streams and processes	Analysis here could include: • Process maturity;

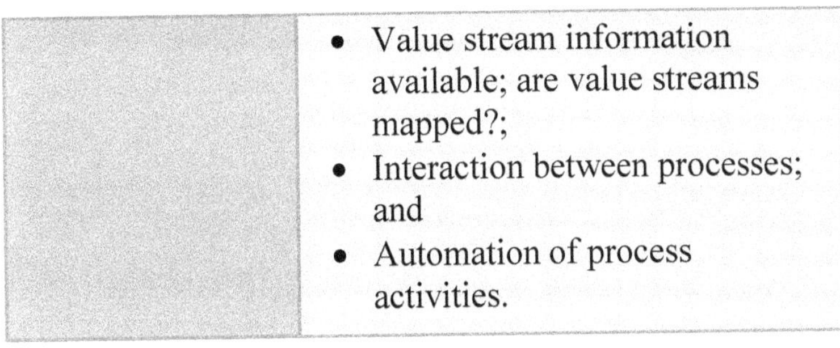

	• Value stream information available; are value streams mapped?; • Interaction between processes; and • Automation of process activities.

During internal analysis, those responsible for strategic planning need to ask:

- *"What capabilities do we need to fulfil the identified needs?*
- *What knowledge would we need?*
- *Which people would we need to hire?*
- *What technology would we need to invest in?*
- *What unique characteristics does the organization have that enable it to fulfil needs in a way that cannot be easily copied by competitors?*
- *Would we need to work with other organizations?*
- *What are our constraints? (What are we unable to do, or what are we able to do in one way but not in another way?)*
- *How should we organize ourselves?*
- *What is the best way of working to fulfil the identified needs?"*

Tools and techniques that support internal analysis include lifecycle analysis, scenario planning and skills matrices. There is more information about each of these in Table 8.

Table 8: Internal analysis tools

Tool	Description/use
Lifecycle analysis	Typically used to analyse the environmental impact through its full lifecycle, this technique can help an organisation make sustainable choices in areas from design to distribution and disposal.
Scenario planning	This allows an organisation to pose 'what if?' questions and see what outcomes would result. For example, what if inflation increased to 10%, or what if we moved our manufacturing offshore? The output from scenario planning will vary in accuracy depending on the input information.
Skills matrix	Skills matrices are used to identify skills and knowledge in an organisation and can be used to support gap analysis and planning for recruitment, training and education.

The organisation and its environment

Change is happening all the time, and most change is unpredictable. It's important to continually monitor and analyse the internal and external environments so that the strategy can be adapted to meet any changes.

Most organisations now accept that their environment is becoming more unpredictable. This doesn't mean we stop planning for the future, but we do need to accept that our plans may change due to circumstances beyond our control (and beyond our current scenarios). Globally, organisations have had to cope with a pandemic that has affected every element of how they operate. In the UK, where I write, inflation spiked in 2022 and 2023, and during the 2022 winter we had energy supply instability related to conflict.

The way that I've approached this with my (small) businesses is to focus on our organisational capabilities to be ready for whatever happens, accepting that we can't foresee everything. We know what we want to achieve as an organisation, and our focus is on building the resilience and adaptability in our supply network that will allow us to meet our goals in spite of what's happening around us. This includes global sourcing, scalable and flexible contracts, and a digital-first approach to everything we do.

What can your organisation do to become more resilient?

Hopefully, environmental analysis will confirm that the organisation's strategy is correct and it is heading in the right direction. Even if this is the case, it's important to continually assess and improve the strategy to meet any new challenges or changing needs. Remember that effective environmental analysis helps an organisation to identify and articulate:

- *"The purpose of the organization*
- *The nature of its interactions with its environment*
- *The products and services it offers, and the needs that each one fulfils*
- *The size of the needs it will fulfill*
- *The constraints imposed by its environment*
- *The capabilities it will need*
- *How it will organize itself to fulfil its purpose (e.g., its business model)*
- *Who it will need to cooperate with"*

CHAPTER 4: DIGITAL AND IT STRATEGY, DIGITAL DISRUPTION AND ORGANISATIONAL VIABILITY

In this chapter, we'll study how an organisation uses Digital and IT Strategy to remain viable in environments that are being disrupted by digital technology. This chapter includes:

- The relationship between organisational viability, agility and resilience;
- Digital and IT Strategy in a VUCA environment;
- The three levels of digital disruption;
- Influencing an organisational position; and
- Digital positioning tools.

The relationship between organisational viability, agility and resilience

An organisation's mission, vision and the resulting business model all help to deliver the required levels of agility and resilience. An organisation needs to be able to adapt to change, but at the same time remain true to its purpose – jumping around from one idea to another can be counter-productive if it doesn't meet overall objectives.

Organisations can adapt their strategy, products and services in response to changes in their environments, but it's important not to lose sight of their purpose and vision.

It could make sense, for example, for a manufacturer of alcoholic drinks to add low and no-alcohol drinks to its product range in response to changing consumer behaviour. But would it make sense for them to move into blockchain? In 2017, Long Island Iced Tea Corp. renamed itself to Long Blockchain Corp., sending its share price to new highs. In April 2018, its shares were delisted from NASDAQ and it announced it would no longer be exploring blockchain-related initiatives. In July 2021, the SEC announced charges of insider trading against three major Long Blockchain investors.[13]

Organisational agility is defined as *"an organization's ability to move and adapt quickly, flexibly, and decisively in response to events in the internal or external environment"*. Organisational resilience is defined as *"an organization's ability to anticipate, prepare for, respond to, and overcome adverse events in the internal or external environment"*.

An agile organisation can make the changes necessary to adapt when circumstances demand resilience.

So, what do we mean by viability? The dictionary defines it as the ability to survive or work successfully. So, for a business to be viable, it needs to fulfil its organisational objectives and remain in a position that allows it to continue. The definition of 'viability' will vary from organisation to organisation – some organisations are founded with the intention of lasting for hundreds of years. Other

[13] https://en.wikipedia.org/wiki/Long_Blockchain_Corp.

organisations are created with an exit in mind – perhaps for founders to sell after a short period. The goals of the business will affect how it defines viability and how that translates into its vision, mission and strategy.

For all organisations, viability can be affected by their internal and external environments, customers' needs/demand and the rate of change. The techniques we've already studied allow organisations to understand these changes, and they can then update their strategy and apply changes in direction or course corrections as needed.

Some changes that organisations experience are fairly minor and easy to absorb – for example, the government changes the law to allow staff to contribute more of their salary into their pensions. Some changes are much more significant, harder to predict and harder to know how to react to. These disruptive events can make or break an organisation. They might lead to total collapse, or they could result in a leaner, more agile organisation that is ready to embrace new challenges. The content we'll study in this chapter relates to how organisations respond effectively to disruptive events.

Digital and IT Strategy in a VUCA environment

Many countries experience significant weather events – often they are referred to as once in a lifetime floods, or fires, or droughts. As the climate changes, these 'once in a lifetime events' are becoming much more frequent, and as a society our responses need to change. Business change and technology change are following similar patterns. The level of change is increasing, and it can feel almost impossible to keep up. The US Army War College created the concept of VUCA, which has been adopted in the business environment. VUCA is defined as:

- **Volatility** – the speed of change;
- **Uncertainty** – the lack of predictability;
- **Complexity** – the number of issues and the amount of confusion related to them; and
- **Ambiguity** – the lack of clarity and potential to misunderstand the situation.

One of my first jobs was in retail at a furniture shop. We took payments in cash, by cheque and by card. Sometimes, the card processing systems would break down. When this happened, we had a stack of paper forms and a machine that we could use to take an imprint of a card. We wrote in all the information by hand, and the transactions were manually keyed in once the systems were back online. Similarly, when I first worked on a helpdesk, we had paper forms we could use when the IT systems were unavailable, and the difference to the customer was negligible.

The complexity of our products and services today means that manual workarounds are pretty much impossible. The amount of digitisation means that we experience change differently as organisations. We need to plan much more carefully to adapt to our VUCA world, because we don't have the old systems to fall back on.

Increased levels of digitisation and the integration of technology into business processes introduce new factors to consider in a VUCA world:

- *"The changing role of technology competency in business management*
- *The increasing pace of competition*
- *Disruptive digitally native competitors*
- *The changing roles of IT management and IT teams in business*
- *The increasing significance of data quality and effective data management*
- *New legislation and requirements in areas such as privacy and information security*
- *IT management practices expanding into various business areas*
- *The return to or introduction of in-house software development*
- *New dependencies on third parties, such as providers of cloud and communication services"*

These factors are often addressed as part of a 'digital transformation strategy'. An organisation's level of maturity in terms of digitisation will affect its ability to respond to these factors effectively.

So, we understand VUCA. But what about BANI, RUPT or TUNA? As the complexity and uncertainty surrounding organisations grows, new models are developed to try to help manage the situation.

- **BANI:** brittle, anxious, non-linear, incomprehensible.
- **RUPT:** rapid, unpredictable, paradoxical, tangled.
- **TUNA:** turbulent, uncertain, novel, ambiguous.

So, which of these is right, or best? The answer is they're all right, and none of them are 'best'. The challenge for us all now as service management practitioners is to understand our environment, understand the tools we have and apply the one that is the best fit for our and our organisation's situation. One of these might resonate with your customer more than the other, perhaps because it aligns with the organisational language. Embrace the idea of lifelong learning and keep your knowledge up to date, but don't let it overwhelm you.

VUCA and the service economy

One area where complexity has increased is the business ecosystem of supply and demand. A service organisation has both service consumers (demand) and service providers (supply) to manage.

An organisation's sourcing strategy will define how it chooses to work with service providers – whether to insource or outsource, whether to work with one service provider or multiple service providers, whether to use long-term, multi-year contracts or 'hire in' services in a more ad hoc way. In the technology world, we also need to consider the many flavours of 'as a service' – Software as a Service, Platform as a Service, Infrastructure as a Service, etc. The challenges associated with the service economy include:

- Increased dependencies, some of which may be hard to control;
- Complex sourcing models;
- An inability to measure end-to-end services or value streams across multiple service providers;
- Increased exposure to external factors (think about PESTLE and Porter); and
- The application of service thinking to traditional 'goods'-based business models.

Understanding these challenges is the first step in preparing an organisation to respond to them.

Using Banksbest or your own organisation, think about how VUCA factors affect the overall strategy and goals. Look at both digital transformation effects and the overall service economy.

Here's an example to get you started. For uncertainty, the digital transformation concern is that technology decisions are hard to make when technology is changing and its role in supporting the business in the future is unclear. From a service economy point of view, there is uncertainty around some of Banksbest's suppliers (MortSys, for example) that can affect its strategic goals.

For each VUCA element, try to document at least one digital transformation and one service economy impact.

So, how does an organisation survive in a VUCA world? Here are some recommendations:

- **Volatility** – be ready for variations – perhaps have more slack in existing resources, or have scalable contracts with service providers.
- **Uncertainty** – maximise use of the information that exists through effective knowledge management.
- **Complexity** – support organisational agility and empower staff at all levels to make decisions.
- **Ambiguity** – experiment and test different options.

Table 9 shows how the ITIL® 4 guiding principles map to the VUCA challenges.

Table 9: Recommendations for acting in a VUCA environment mapped to the seven guiding principles[14]

Characteristic	*Focus on value*	*Start where you are*	*Progress iteratively with feedback*	*Collaborate and promote visibility*	*Think and work holistically*	*Keep it simple and practical*	*Optimize and automate*
Volatility	X		X	X	X	X	
Uncertainty	X	X	X			X	X
Complexity	X		X	X	X		

[14] *ITIL® 4: Digital and IT Strategy*, Table 8.3. ITIL® is a registered trade mark of the PeopleCert group. Used under licence from PeopleCert. All rights reserved.

Ambiguity	*X*		*X*	*X*	*X*		

The *ITIL® 4: High-velocity IT* publication describes five behaviour patterns:

- Accept ambiguity and uncertainty.
- Trust and be trusted.
- Continually raise the bar.
- Help get customers' jobs done.
- Commit to continual learning.

These can also be of value when applied to the VUCA challenges. Accept ambiguity and uncertainty doesn't require much further explanation, but it's worth considering the application of the other behaviours. The table below provides more information.

Table 10: HVIT behaviour patterns and VUCA

Behaviour pattern	VUCA applicability
Trust and be trusted	Trust enables autonomy and personal accountability. This can help organisations react more quickly to changes.
Continually raise the bar	A commitment to raise the bar (rather than think 'but we've always done it

	that way'!) can help an organisation respond to changes and be proactive.
Help get customers' jobs done	If everyone is focused on value and value to the customer, changes can be assessed in this light, making it easier to identify the correct action(s) to take.
Commit to continual learning	The more we know, the more tools we have when the need arises.

Figure 11 shows the five characteristics for operating in a VUCA environment.

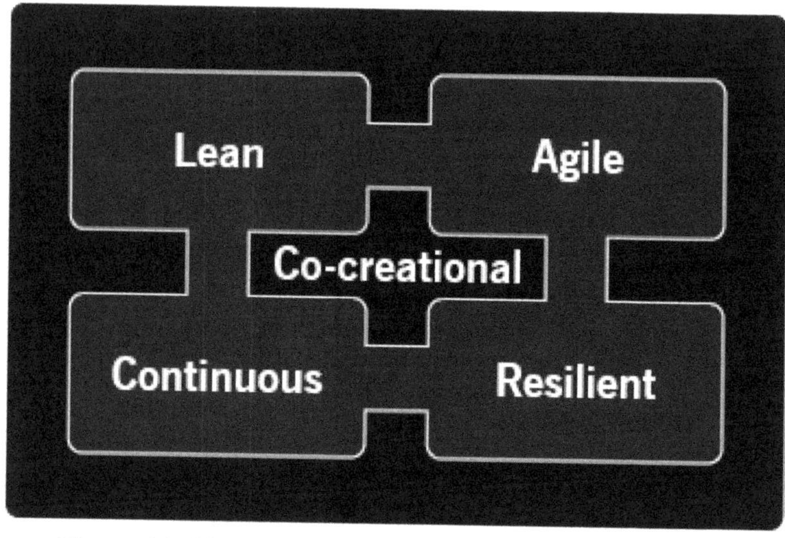

Figure 11: Five characteristics for operating in a VUCA environment[15]

Organisations that are lean, agile, resilient and continuous are likely to be able to deliver value in an ever-changing world. **Agility** allows them to move quickly and be flexible when required. **Resilience** means they are prepared for changes and external disruptions, and have the ability to respond. **Lean** organisations are focused on value for the customer, delivered in the most efficient way. **Continuous** means that an organisation can provide uninterrupted, predictable services, even when its environment is changing.

[15] *ITIL® 4: Digital and IT Strategy*, Figure 8.2. ITIL® is a registered trade mark of the PeopleCert group. Used under licence from PeopleCert. All rights reserved.

Strategic methods to address VUCA

So, how does an organisation embrace the VUCA environment? It starts with the strategy. The organisation needs to create awareness of its environment and develop appropriate behaviours.

Volatility planning will include digital and IT strategies that address survival. Organisations need to plan for potential budget cuts, funding projects, programmes, knowledge-sharing, communication, succession planning and decision-making when necessary. Volatility planning needs to include the cuts necessary when demand decreases, but also a plan to rebuild once demand rebounds. Volatility may also include a spike in demand, and plans need to address scalability from this perspective as well.

Uncertainty planning is enabled or limited by an organisation's 'absorptive capacity'. This is defined in ITIL® 4 as the *"ability to recognize the value of new information, embed it into an existing knowledge system, and apply it to achieve the business outcomes"*. Effective knowledge management will underpin planning for uncertainty.

Complexity can only be addressed by understanding the context. If the context is misinterpreted, the wrong solution may be applied. Cynefin, shown in Figure 12, is a widely adopted framework for assessing complexity and defining appropriate actions.

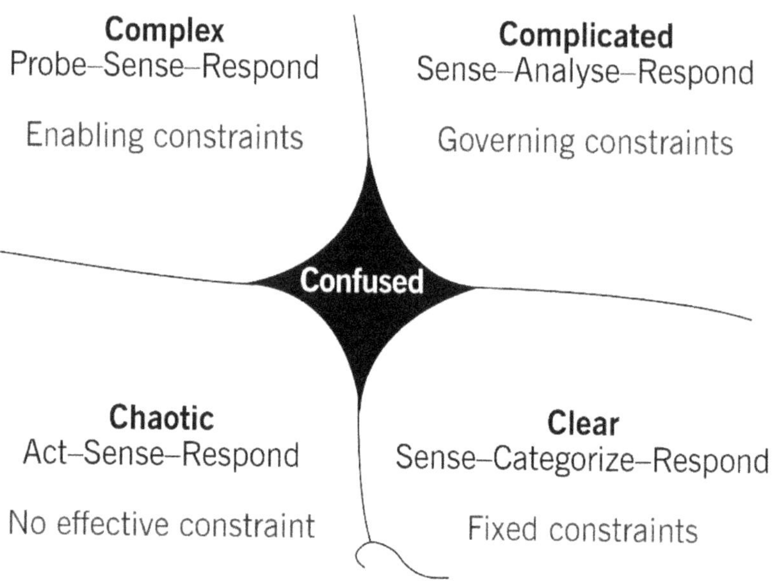

Figure 12: The Cynefin framework[16]

The five Cynefin domains are clear, complicated, chaotic, complex and confused. The framework helps people use the most appropriate approach for the situation.

[16] *ITIL® 4: Digital and IT Strategy*, Figure 8.3. ITIL® is a registered trade mark of the PeopleCert group. Used under licence from PeopleCert. All rights reserved. Also courtesy of The Cynefin Company. *https://thecynefin.co*.

For this exercise, you can use the Banksbest case study or your own organisation if you have a similar scenario you can use.

Lucy at Banksbest has been made aware of two incidents relating to the My Way project. In the first incident, a customer has been unable to deposit a cheque using their phone because of a permission error on their mobile device. In the second incident, a pilot of a biometric service has led to a customer being shown someone else's account information when they logged in using their fingerprint.

Using Cynefin, think about the response to both of these incidents. How are they different? How would the response need to change?

Ambiguity planning needs to reflect the fact that it can be hard to identify the best action to take.

The Toyota Kata can also be used to create a mental model for scientific thinking and address ambiguity. It supports experimentation and needs to be used within a 'safety culture' where staff are empowered to take action and don't feel frightened of failure or punishment. Figure 13 shows the steps in the Toyota Kata:

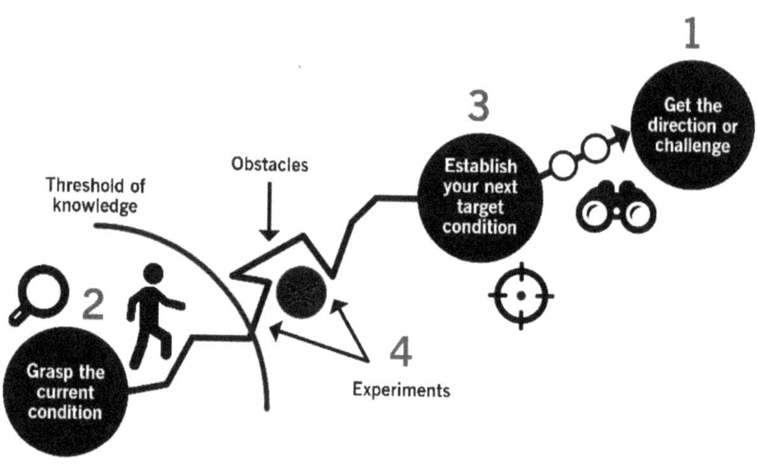

Figure 13: Toyota improvement kata[17]

The steps in the kata are:

- Get the direction/challenge – aim at specific goals;
- Grasp the current condition with a baseline measure;
- Establish the next target condition and understand the expected conditions necessary to achieve the goal; and
- Experiment towards the next target by generating ideas to overcome any obstacles and then experimenting.

Levels of digital disruption

Disruption occurs when an organisation's operation experiences a fundamental shift caused by an internal or external factor. The ITIL® 4: Digital and IT Strategy

[17] *ITIL® 4: Digital and IT Strategy*, Figure 8.4. From Rother, M. (2018). The Toyota Kata Practice Guide. McGraw Hill. ITIL® is a registered trade mark of the PeopleCert group. Used under licence from PeopleCert. All rights reserved.

publication is focused on disruption caused by digital technology. Successful organisations will react effectively to disruption, and may use digital technology to disrupt their own environment, giving them an advantage.

There are three possible levels of disruption: ecosystem level, industry or market level, and organisation level. We'll review these in more detail now.

Ecosystem disruption

An ecosystem disruption takes place when digital technology introduces a change that affects multiple organisations, industries and markets. An example would be Airbnb, which used its platform to disrupt the hotel industry across the world by connecting people with space to rent with people who wanted to rent. If an organisation wants to disrupt an ecosystem, it must use disruptive digital technologies across the business, and in multiple market segments and/or industries.

Industry disruption

Industry disruption occurs when digital technology introduces a change to a specific industry or to a group of related industries. Often, industry disruption is a side effect of an organisation pursuing operational efficiencies, rather than the end goal. For example, the use of chatbots and AI to deliver support and allow organisations to 'shift left' has created disruption across the customer service industry.

If an organisation wishes to disrupt an industry, it will need to use technology to compete more effectively and to grow market share. It may attempt to bankrupt or acquire its competitors. An organisation could also create an entity that will sell the new technology to competitors as products or services.

Disruptive technology will not necessarily create long-lasting competitive advantage, as other organisations copy and build on new ideas.

Market disruption

Market disruption occurs when digital technology affects a specific market or market segment. As with industry disruption, market disruption is usually a result of:

- Improving the delivery mechanism;
- Improving products and services;
- Improving customer engagement models; and/or
- Duplicating success in one market to another.

Organisational disruption

Most organisations are not disruptive in themselves. They have established markets, products, services, operations, etc. They will experience disruption in their markets that they will need to respond to in order to recover or maintain their position. When digital technology disrupts their environment or their market, organisations will often adopt the new technology to maintain their level of competitiveness. This creates disruption within the organisation. If an organisation is successful (or early) when adopting a new technology, it may become a market leader and develop a more innovative culture.

Figure 14 shows two possible ways disruption can occur.

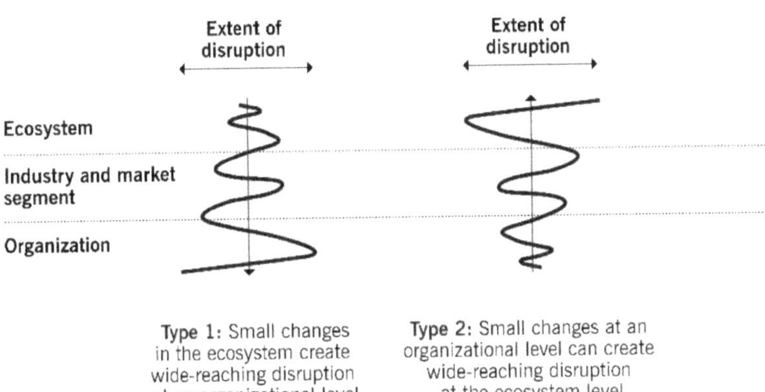

Figure 14: Types of disruption[18]

Influencing an organisational position

There are different approaches an organisation can take if it wishes to disrupt an industry. It may focus on customer or market relevance with unique products and services, or it may focus on operational excellence to deliver cheaper and/or better products and services.

Customer/market relevance approaches can include:

- Changing the customer experience, journey or behaviour;
- Influencing demand;
- Organisational engagement; and

[18] *ITIL® 4: Digital and IT Strategy*, Figure 3.2 ITIL® is a registered trade mark of the PeopleCert group. Used under licence from PeopleCert.

- Market innovation: creating new markets or transforming an existing one.

Ideally, an organisation will focus on both areas – customer/market relevance and operational excellence. The two areas are interrelated and interdependent. It will be harder for an organisation to achieve competitive differentiation if it only focuses on one.

For this exercise, you can focus on Banksbest or you can use your own current or a previous organisation. If you're using Banksbest, look at the different initiatives that are taking place. Which of them are related to operational excellence, and which are related to innovation? Why? Do you feel it has a good balance?

If you're using your own organisation, use the same approach to assess any projects or programmes that are underway and which area they are linked to.

To fully understand an organisation's position requires a holistic focus that includes internal and external elements. You can see the elements to focus on in Table 11. The answers to these questions will allow an organisation to create its digital vision.

Table 11: Internal/external focus questions

Internal focus	External focus
"What do we need to do to continue doing business? *What do we need to do differently?* *How do we manage the risk associated with each opportunity?* *How do we monitor and control our journey?* *How can we improve operational efficiencies?* *How can we reduce costs?* *How do we get to where we want to be?"*	*"What markets do we serve?* *What products and services do we currently provide to the market? Are they valuable?* *What opportunities are there for growth or disruption? What threats do we face?* *What capabilities do we have that open new avenues for us in existing or new markets?"*

The strategy that an organisation creates needs to balance customer needs/market relevance and operational excellence. Focusing on one area may create waste. New products and services will only add value if they are supported by effective operations. Improving operations will only add value if there is demand for the products and services the organisation offers. A balanced strategic approach based on small, incremental changes is more likely to be effective and to help an organisation reach its strategic goals.

This table shows some examples of how an organisation can identify improvements in a balanced way, looking at both internal and external drivers.

Table 12: Looking outwards vs looking inwards[19]

	Looking outwards	***Looking inwards***
Customer/market relevance	*How are customer needs changing?* *What products and services will they need?* *How will they procure and use them?* *What opportunities are emerging?* *How easy will it be to do business with the organization?* *What PESTLE (political, economic, social, technological, legal, or environmental)*	*How do we engage with customers?* *How do customers experience the way we deliver products and services?* *How do our employees and technology support the customer experience?* *What will we need in order to exploit new opportunities?*

[19] *ITIL® 4: Digital and IT Strategy*, Table 3.2. ITIL® is a registered trade mark of the PeopleCert group. Used under licence from PeopleCert. All rights reserved.

	factors need to be considered?	
Operational excellence	*How do other organizations perform?* *What technologies do they use?* *How much do they spend on running their business?* *What PESTLE factors need to be considered?*	*What are our capabilities?* *Is there a better way of running the business?* *Can we use technology more effectively and efficiently?* *How will performance need to improve over time?*

Positioning tools for digital organisations

The tools we'll consider in this section can be used to evaluate digital opportunities, support decision-making, and support strategy creation and development. There are many tools available to organisations; choosing the correct tool(s) to apply from the range of maturity models and digital positioning models available can be a challenge in its own right.

Organisations need to understand:

- Their ecosystem, market(s) and industries;

- The appropriate level and balance of customer/market relevance and operational excellence;
- What opportunities to exploit;
- The value proposition for their targeted markets, industries and consumers;
- Products and services; and
- Which business model to use.

The pace of change in digital markets means that there is no one 'best' way to create a digital model or map a position. We'll look at two major approaches – maturity models, and digital positioning and sense making.

Maturity models

Maturity models are based on the theory that there is a set of characteristics that increase the chances of an organisation being successful. There are two main types of maturity model:

- **Models focused on organisational characteristics:** for example, Westerman et al. (2014) assesses an organisation based on two dimensions (digital capabilities and leadership capabilities), which then lead on to four quadrants – beginners, fashionistas, conservatives and digital masters.
- **Models focused on moving from one level to another:** for example, helping an organisation to move from one level of disruption (e.g. organisational) to the next – market, industry or ecosystem.

Figure 15 gives more detail about the maturity model focused on organisational characteristics:

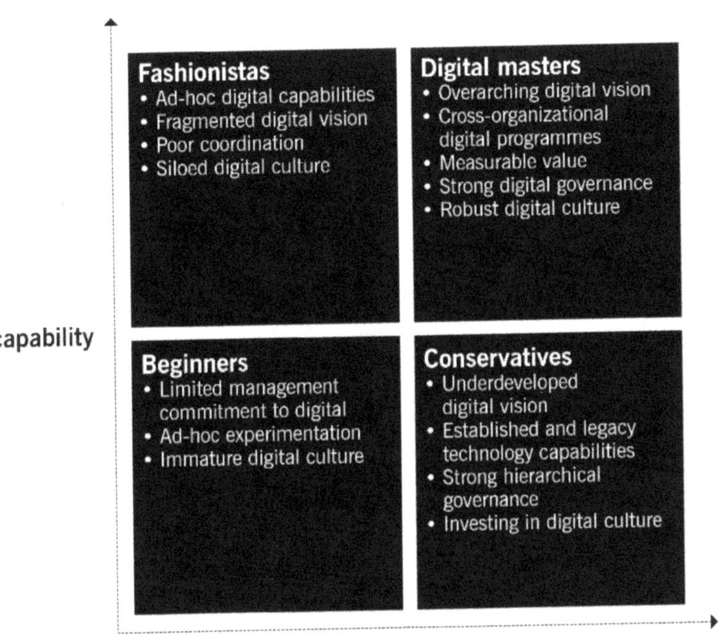

Figure 15: Four types of digital master, Westerman 2014[20]

Maturity models do have limitations. In a disruptive digital environment where changes are happening quickly, they can be time consuming and may lead to an organisation focusing on the wrong variables.

---

[20] *ITIL® 4: Digital and IT Strategy*, Figure 3.3. From Westerman, G., Bonnet, D. and McAfee, A. (2014) Leading Digital: Turning Technology into Business Transformation. Havard Business Review Press. ITIL® is a registered trade mark of the PeopleCert group. Used under licence from PeopleCert. All rights reserved.

Some organisations use maturity models as a 'quick fix' in place of doing more rigorous strategic planning and analysis. This can lead to problems if:

- The maturity model is based on analysis of multiple organisations, not tailored to the organisation using it;
- The definition of success is not clear, or the authors of the model had a different definition of success; and/or
- The organisation is engaged in innovative activities that are not yet reflected in available models.

The main issue that I've experienced with organisations using maturity models is the model becomes the goal. Rather than an indicator of their current level of progress, many organisations pick the level they think they 'should' be at and then spend hours putting corrections in place to get them to where they want to be. Some organisations that I've worked with have been afraid to reassess a particular area of the business, because their last rating was good and they know things have got worse since then. A maturity rating is an indication of where an organisation is, not a judgement on how good or bad they are. The rating should be seen as a positive, no matter what level it is, and any improvement opportunities highlighted should be assessed and cost-justified. Unless your entire business survival depends on getting a 'level 3', you don't need to waste resources moving up from level 2.

Digital positioning models and sensemaking

Figure 16 shows an example of a digital positioning assessment framework.

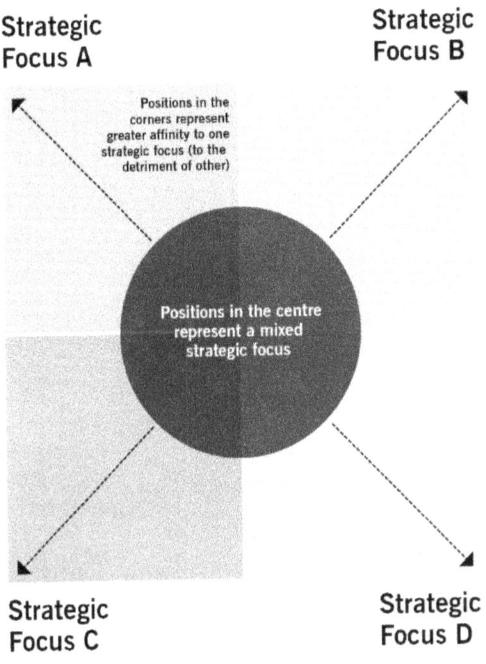

Figure 16: Digital positioning assessment framework[21]

The framework can be used for one organisation or for a group of competitors. A cluster of competitors within the model defines a 'zone of competition'. If this is crowded, an organisation may choose to leave the zone, or revise its

---

[21] *ITIL® 4: Digital and IT Strategy*, Figure 3.4. ITIL® is a registered trade mark of the PeopleCert group. Used under licence from PeopleCert.

strategic goals to create greater differentiation. The framework can also show how an organisation's position will change as it achieves its strategic goals.

The next positioning model (Figure 17) provides an organisation with a way to assess its position against different strategic focus areas such as consumer/market relevance, operational excellence, industry disruption or transformation, or market disruption or transformation.

The figure shows a cluster in customer experience and operational excellence, so organisations in this zone of competition may have to re-evaluate their position to look for a way to differentiate themselves.

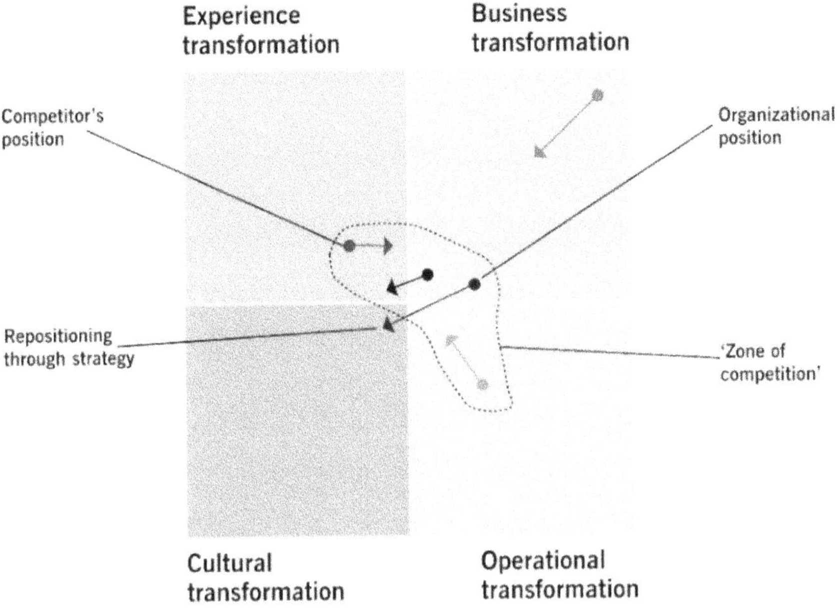

Figure 17: Positioning assessment framework focused on business, operational, cultural and experience transformation[22]

An organisation could also assess itself against different focus areas from its digital strategy, such as:

- Physical presence;
- Digital presence;
- Use of emerging technologies; and
- Use of industry-standard tools and technologies.

[22] *ITIL® 4: Digital and IT Strategy*, Figure 3.5. ITIL® is a registered trade mark of the PeopleCert group. Used under licence from PeopleCert.

Figure 18 shows how a change in strategic focus will move an organisation to a different position, as well as changing its direction of travel.

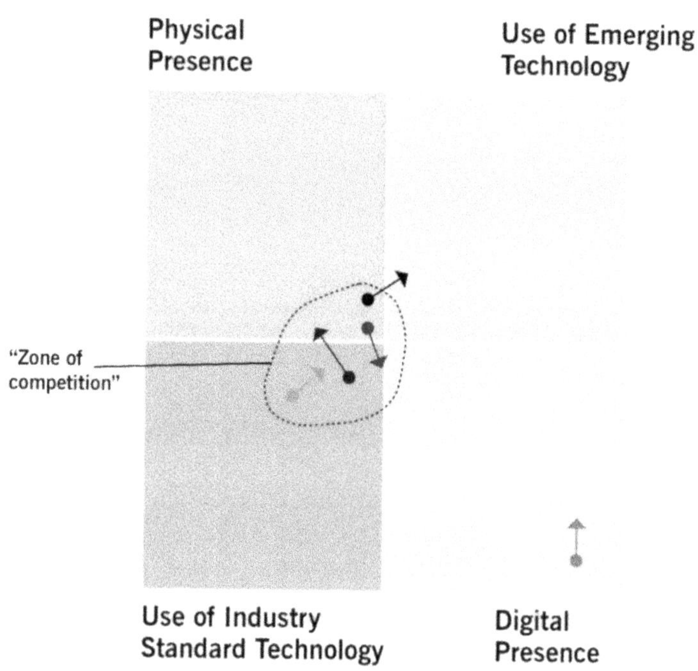

Figure 18: Positioning assessment framework focused on physical and digital presence, and the use of emerging and standard technologies[23]

Mapping maturity and digital positioning is not a one-off exercise. It should be revisited regularly as the organisation's ecosystem evolves.

---

[23] *ITIL® 4: Digital and IT Strategy*, Figure 3.6. ITIL® is a registered trade mark of the PeopleCert group. Used under licence from PeopleCert. All rights reserved.

Here's an exercise for you to complete. Using the Banksbest case study, think of three examples of digital disruptions that could potentially affect the organisation. You may want to do some research online into fintech if you're not familiar with the financial industry, or you may be able to draw on your own experience.

CHAPTER 5: APPROACHES TO ACHIEVE MARKET RELEVANCE AND OPERATIONAL EXCELLENCE

In this chapter, we'll consider the different strategic approaches made possible by digital and information technology to achieve customer/market relevance and operational excellence. The chapter includes these key approaches:

- Customer journey.
- Omnichannel delivery and support.
- Context-sensitive delivery and support.
- Customer analytics.
- Customer feedback and 360-degree approaches.

It also covers approaches to achieve operational excellence and the financial aspects of Digital and IT Strategy, and strategic approaches for digital organisations. The chapter then explains information from the service financial management and portfolio management practices.

Key strategic approaches for digital organisations

The strategy of a digital organisation reflects its values and its business model, and needs to balance customer and market relevance with operational excellence. Customer needs change over time, so what is right today won't necessarily do the job tomorrow. The Barrett model (Figure

19) describes organisational values, and can be used to define an organisation's strategic focus.[24]

[24] *ITIL® 4: Digital and IT Strategy*, Figure 5.3. ITIL® is a registered trade mark of the PeopleCert group. Used under licence from PeopleCert.

Contribution	7	**Living purpose** Being of service, future generations, vision, social responsibility, long-term perspective.
Collaboration	6	**Cultivating communities** Community involvement, partnership, mentoring/coaching, employee fulfilment.
Alignment	5	**Authentic expression** Openness, creativity, integrity, passion, trust, honesty, transparency.
Evolution	4	**Courageously evolving** Accountability, transformation, innovation, continuous learning, autonomy, empowerment, agility.
Performance	3	**Achieving excellence** Quality, results-orientation, competence, self-esteem, productivity, efficiency.
Relationships	2	**Building relationships** Customer satisfaction, connection, respect, listening, open communication.
Viability	1	**Ensuring stability** Financial stability, profit, safety, health.

Figure 5.3 The Barrett model

Reproduced with permission from the Barrett Values Centre (2020).

Figure 19: The Barrett model

To achieve customer relevance, organisations need to be able to *"continually meet and exceed customer expectations, and changes to their customer and their context"*. Because customer needs change over time, an organisation that provides products and services must understand value from the customers' perspective.

McCarthy (1960) defined a four Ps approach to the customer perspective: product, price, promotion and place. In 1990, Lauterborn created a more consumer-focused four Cs approach: consumer needs, cost, communication and convenience.

Not every organisation is profit-seeking or part of the private sector. Organisations like non-profit, government, etc. will also need to understand their consumers and what value means for them.

Market relevance is defined in ITIL 4 as *"the ability to continue to operate within a market that is characterized by a particular use of digital technology, and how that technology and its use changes"*.

Maintaining market relevance requires an organisation to be flexible and agile as its market evolves. The next sections in this chapter define some approaches, tools and techniques that can help an organisation understand and maintain its customer and market relevance.

Customer journey

A customer journey is defined in ITIL® 4 as *"the complete end-to-end experience that service customers have with one or more service providers and/or their products though touchpoints and service interactions"*.

An organisation needs to understand why a customer chooses to engage. What is the customer trying to achieve? How do they use the product/services that the service provider offers? Once an organisation understands more about its customer, it can provide a solution focused on meeting their needs. 'Design thinking' is one approach that can be used to ensure that a product/service is built with the customer in mind.

There have been two major changes during my career in service management that really help organisations understand and meet customer needs.

The first change is the move to online services. As customers (or potential customers) engage with digital services, we can collect huge amounts of information about what they want and what they do. We can test different versions of a service simultaneously, and track every movement of a customer's mouse should we wish to.

The second change is the move from waterfall to Agile development. Waterfall is still absolutely appropriate for some IT projects and programmes, but the iterative approach that Agile offers makes it much easier to adjust course as we understand more about our customer's requirements. Think about how you develop products and services in your own organisation, or at a previous employer. Was the customer involved from the start?

A customer journey map is a useful tool to understand more about the customer's experience with a particular product or service. Figure 20 shows an example of a map.[25]

[25] *ITIL® 4: Digital and IT Strategy*, Figure 5.8. ITIL® is a registered trade mark of the PeopleCert group. Used under licence from PeopleCert. All rights reserved.

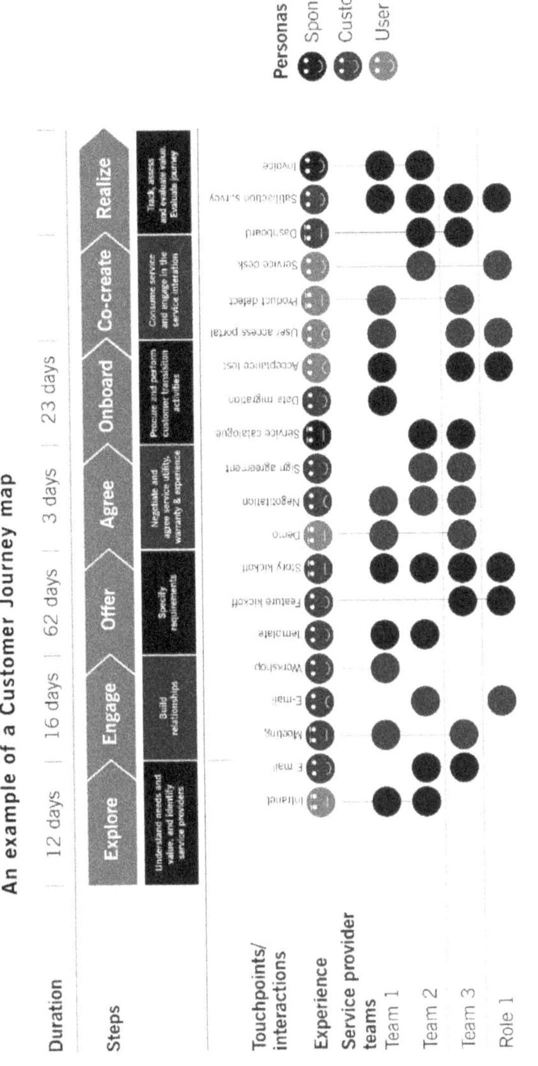

Figure 20: Example of a customer journey map

A customer journey map can be used to understand a customer's experience with an existing product or service, or to design the desired experience for a new/planned product or service. The map helps define any gaps between the desired experience and reality.

The key elements of a map are:

- **Persona:** a sketch of the customer or user who will make the journey;
- **Journey steps:** including wait times;
- Thoughts and feelings: both positive and negative;
- **Touchpoints:** interactions between people, technology, services, value streams, etc.;
- **Underlying ecosystem:** capturing the organisations, tools and policies that contribute to the perceived experience and their effectiveness; and
- **Current state vs future state:** how the service is perceived today and predicted experiences based on personas.

For this exercise, use your own knowledge and the Banksbest case study to create two customer journey maps.

Map 1: the existing experience for a customer depositing a cheque at a bank.

Map 2: the experience for a customer depositing a cheque via their mobile phone.

What are the key differences between the two maps? Does the new service introduce any risks?

Omnichannel delivery and support

An omnichannel approach can help an organisation achieve operational excellence and maintain its customer/market relevance. Omnichannel delivers a seamless experience, allowing customer engagement across multiple communication and delivery channels. Implemented correctly, it delivers a consistent and positive customer experience.

The channel types can be direct (where a customer engages directly with a service provider, for example through website, email and chat) or indirect (where a third party provides an intermediary service, for example a reseller or an outsourced helpdesk).

To deliver an effective omnichannel experience, an organisation needs to address the following:

- **Digital customer experience** – focus on customer interactions to ensure a positive experience; develop appropriate interaction mediums.
- **Digital operational excellence** – focus on the ecosystem required to deliver the customer experience; manage and integrate internal, partner and third-party services for seamless operations.

Digital technology has a huge impact on an organisation's ability to deliver omnichannel support. Think about, for example, how you interact with your bank via your phone (voice), your phone (app) or your PC, and in a branch.

Context-sensitive delivery and support

Understanding the context of all interactions can help an organisation tailor its approach to its customers, based on their needs. Providing a tailored, rather than generic, service encourages customer engagement.

Digital customer support can be challenging. When someone is having a bad time already, getting trapped in an endless list of automated options can make their day worse. If we don't have a human connection by putting two people together, as service providers we still need to try to create an empathetic and appropriate service.

For example, many service providers now have a specific path to inform them of a bereavement. The UK government has a 'tell us once' service that allows a user to report a death to most government organisations through one form.

There are three key elements to develop a context-sensitive approach:

- **Evaluate interactions** – ideally, use omnichannel to get a broad spectrum of information on the customer and understand patterns of interaction.

- **Build feedback mechanisms** – develop feedback loops (data) in products and services so data is 'real time' to allow effective responses.
- **Develop analytical capabilities** – develop analytic skills for a more data-driven decision to improve the overall experience.

Customer analytics

It sounds obvious that we should make decisions based on what our customers want. But many organisations struggle to do this, and make decisions based on their perception of their customers. This can be very different to the truth. Digital technology gives us access to a wealth of data that can be used to drive better decision-making, for example:

- How and why do customers use our services?
- What demand is there for new products and/or services?
- What gaps do we have, for example in our portfolio or performance?

This customer data can be correlated with external and environmental factors. For example, in a recession a service provider may see customers switch from premium to budget services, or cancel their subscriptions.

Customer feedback and 360-degree approaches

Customer 360 is not a new concept, but digital technology has increased the amount of data available to us when we apply it.

Customer 360 builds a holistic view of a customer based on multiple data sources, for example purchase history, support contacts, reviews left on social media, and so on. Analysing a 360 view of its customers allows an organisation to adapt or create products and services in a way that is truly aligned with customer wants and needs. This can deepen customer loyalty, giving an organisation competitive advantage.

Customer feedback provides real-time information that can be analysed to help maintain customer relevance. New and changed products and services can be developed based on an enhanced understanding of customer needs. Tools like customer satisfaction surveys and Net Promoter Score can highlight positives and any issues or gaps that need to be addressed. Face-to-face workshops and focus groups can then be used to gain further insight and look at the 'why' that is attached to a customer's view.

More and more organisations that I work with are shifting their focus to experience and measuring how their customers feel about their products and services. Experience measures give us a very different perspective to that provided by traditional service level agreements, and ideally an organisation will use both types of measurement.

Take the example of someone working in finance using a payroll application. It fails on the last working day of the month, when payslips are being produced. It also fails the week after, when there is no payroll activity happening. The service level agreement may show that the application has performed within the agreed limits for downtime. But ask the person working on it how they feel about the two outages, and you could get a very different response. The impact of the downtime during payroll is much more significant.

If your organisation isn't already acting on this, you may wish to do some research on experience level agreements (XLAs).

Approaches to achieve operational excellence

Operational excellence is necessary to achieve consistent, effective, long-lasting products and services that benefit the consumer. It can be viewed from the perspective of the four dimensions of service management from ITIL® 4, as shown in the table below.

Table 13: Operational excellence and the four dimensions of service management

Dimension	Operational excellence considerations
Organizations and people	Clear roles/responsibilities, a culture of experimentation and continual improvement, governance is defined and balanced, waste is analysed and removed; there is risk-based decision making.
Information and technology	Focus on high-value tasks; automation is deployed for repetitive/low-value tasks; integration across the organisation to increase flow, transparency, information, knowledge.

Partners and suppliers	Enable collaboration, leading to growth, innovation and continual improvement.
Value streams and processes	Identify gaps/waste within value streams; focus on clear, repeatable, scalable, efficient, effective processes and practices.

We'll study a number of possible approaches to achieve operational excellence, including:

- Competitive advantage;
- Continual improvement;
- Automation;
- Service optimisation;
- Technology replacement and modernisation;
- Sourcing strategies;
- Workforce strategies; and
- Employee 360 approaches.

Competitive advantage

Operational excellence isn't just about reducing waste and adding efficiencies. It can be a source of competitive advantage. The table below provides some examples:

Table 14: Operational excellence and competitive advantage

Type of advantage	Link to operational excellence

Scale advantage	This is an advantage based on growing the organisation or the customer base. An organisation can: • Use size to achieve economies of scale; and • Use a platform to dominate customer/provider interactions.
Incumbency advantage	Being first to market or a preferred provider. To compete against an incumbent provider, an organisation needs to have credibility and provide high-quality or specialised products and services.
Resource-based advantage	An organisation has resources that other organisations don't have access to. These resources must be rare or valuable, non-replicable, durable, etc. Patents are a good example.

Continual improvement

Strategies and approaches based on continual improvement are not typically disruptive. Continual improvement doesn't result in radical changes to an organisation; rather, it focuses on how the organisation can maintain its market position and its customer base. It's usually an incremental approach that may leverage innovation and emerging technology, but can also be applied to legacy environments and stable systems.

There are two strategic approaches to address sub-optimal performance in an organisation. The first is based around information and technology modernisation (for example, moving a data centre into the Cloud to achieve performance and efficiency benefits). The second is based around value stream and process improvement (for example, automating process steps or enabling self-service to speed up time to value).

I've worked with organisations that have started multiple transformation projects at the same time. They had a huge focus on dramatic, large-scale interventions, but never had the time or budget to focus on continual improvement. It can be hard to get senior people to buy in to a continual improvement approach; they often ask why we can't just leave things alone if they're working right now. If you have a similar challenge, it can help to link continual improvement to the organisation's strategic objectives. For example, an intelligent hardware refresh programme can help an organisation achieve environmental goals.

Automation

There are many potential applications for automation in the digital environment. From internal process improvements through to customer-facing interactions, automation can speed up transaction times, reduce costs and remove errors associated with manual activities.

Automation can even allow an organisation to offer new products and services, leading to changes in the organisation's strategy, business model and vision.

Automation commoditises activities and decisions, allowing staff to focus on higher-value, more complex work. The table below shows three possible levels of automation.

Table 15: Levels of automation

Level	Description
Simple automation	Simple automation is applied to lower-level actions and decisions, usually frequently performed and well understood. Simple automation will usually reduce cost and/or increase speed, but may not lead to any disruption of the organisation's operations. An example of simple automation could be automating service requests such as getting access to software or ordering a laptop.
Complex automation	Complex automation coordinates multiple simple, related activities or decisions. For example, the employee onboarding process could be automated to include access to software, ordering a laptop, provision of induction training, etc.
Intelligent automation	Intelligent automation performs activities or decisions differently depending on the context. This requires the application of 'intelligence' often using artificial intelligence or decision trees. For example, automating candidate vetting as part of

	recruitment to make decisions about which candidates to interview.

Service optimisation

Service optimisation is a continual improvement strategy that aims to improve either the quality or performance of a service, or both. Products and services need to be assessed against the expected performance to allow optimisation activities to be identified. An organisation will invest in making service optimisation improvements for products and services that support organisational objectives. If the product or service isn't linked to organisational objectives, it may instead be marked for retirement or replacement.

Technology replacement and modernisation

This technique is aimed at replacing or restructuring equipment that is out of date or expensive to maintain. Architecture that no longer supports business objectives can be retired in a controlled way. Overall, the business will aim to improve its performance and efficiency through technology modernisation activities.

Sourcing strategies

Shadow IT is defined as *"the use of IT-related hardware or software by a department or individual without the knowledge of the IT or security group within the organization"*.

Shadow IT exists in many organisations, and may be referred to with negative terms such as fake IT, stealth IT, rogue IT or feral IT. It can also be referred to as client IT or embedded IT, recognising the value of allowing business units to source their own digital solutions.

Each organisation will need to decide how to tackle shadow IT. It can try to remove it, but this can negatively affect the reputation of the IT department and drive purchasing decisions further underground. It's often better to build relationships and provide support to areas of the business that are investing in digital products and services, providing expertise and architectural information. The risk of unmanaged shadow IT is that there is no centrally defined sourcing strategy, leading to potential waste, duplication and poor management.

A digital organisation will need to work closely with its suppliers and needs a sourcing strategy that will:

- Support overall financial strategies;
- Coordinate multiple suppliers that contribute to the same product, service or value stream;
- Provide flexible and scalable contracts; and
- Create a culture of collaboration and build good relationships with suppliers.

Workforce strategies

Workforce strategies will affect operational excellence. Organisations need to think carefully about the skills that they need now and in the future. The entire workforce lifecycle should be carefully managed, from onboarding to ongoing training and development all the way through to offboarding and knowledge transfer when an employee leaves.

Note – you'll find a lot more information on this area in the ITIL® 4 workforce and talent management practice guide.

Employee 360 approaches

The final approach to achieving operational excellence is similar to the customer 360 approach we looked at earlier in this chapter. Digital technology can provide huge amounts of data about employee needs, preferences and behaviours that can be used to improve the working environment. This is particularly useful as more knowledge workers work from home, limiting the amount of in-person interaction. Once an organisation understands more about how its employees work, it can provide tools and resources to optimise the work environment.

The increased focus on employee experience, the rise in home/flexible working and advances in technology have led to a new group of products aimed at measuring employee experience. This is a great idea, but it's important to be transparent about what is being deployed and not be, well, creepy with it. I'm really happy if my employer can tell that an application is crashing on my laptop and it would be a good idea to reinstall it. I don't want my employer monitoring my keystrokes or trying to guess when I'm being productive or not.

I've reworded this slightly, but one company offers software that will let you "see what your employees are up to, every minute of every day". I wouldn't expect someone stood behind me monitoring me in the office, so don't treat me differently at home.

Financial aspects of Digital and IT Strategy

We'll cover some essential information here, but it's also a good idea to read the ITIL® 4 service financial management practice guide.

Financial management is a key capability for any organisation undertaking strategic planning exercises. With a limitless budget, any organisation could do anything, but in reality most of us are working within financial constraints and need to prioritise where we invest. Understanding financial management is a key skillset for anyone in a strategic role.

Every organisation could provide perfect, premium products and services way beyond its customers' expectations if it wanted to. The reason they don't is it's usually not cost-justifiable and could even put them at risk of bankruptcy (for a private-sector organisation). The money that an organisation spends on creating and delivering products and services must be cost-justified and linked to organisational goals and customer needs.

At the same time, an organisation can't meet its goals or customer needs if there isn't enough money available to support products and services. There must be appropriate funding available for the business model, and for new and existing products and services, taking into account any environmental changes that may affect the service budget.

There's a cartoon I see a lot on social media that really makes me laugh. It gives the quote "meh, good enough!" and attributes it to Mediocrates. Good enough is a really important concept that is closely linked to strategic planning and the amount of money that we invest in our products and services. I see a lot of organisations making elaborate statements about wanting to 'delight' their customers, which implies going well beyond customer expectations. Many customers, however, are happy with 'good enough'. Adding too many extra features to our products and services can make them too expensive to justify, and result in only very minor increases in customer satisfaction.

Think about hotel chains – sometimes you pay for luxury and you expect the hotel to deliver. Sometimes you pay a much lower price and your expectations will be lower. If you get a comfy bed and a clean room, does it significantly change your experience if there's no chocolate on the pillow? Meh, it's good enough!

Digital organisations may have a more agile approach to budgeting. Table 16 shows the key differences between agile and 'traditional' funding models.

Table 16: Types of funding strategy

Agile funding strategy	Funding is broken down into smaller budgets, allowing it to be allocated based on the results of each iteration. Funding may be at team level and across multiple value streams.
Traditional funding strategy	More commonly used for large, multi-year project and programmes. This can mean funds are 'tied' to projects and can't be reinvested if there is a new priority.

What type of funding strategy would you recommend for Banksbest? Why? What are the associated benefits and risks of the strategy that you're recommending?

Financial policies

All strategies have some kind of financial component. An organisation may have a goal to achieve financial growth, and it will certainly need funds to deliver its products and services. An organisation may need to borrow to achieve its strategic goals, or it may have surplus cash to invest, perhaps in research and development. PESTLE factors can also impact the financial elements of a strategy, for example tax legislation may affect where an organisation bases itself.

One of the key financial decisions is between a capital and an operational expenditure model. Capital costs are defined as the *"cost of purchasing or creating resources, which are recognized as financial assets (depreciation)"*. Operational costs are *"costs the organization incurs through its normal business operations"*. The decisions an organisation makes about digital products and services can impact the funding model – for example, moving from its own data centre to using a Cloud provider will likely lead to a switch from capital expenditure to operational.

Capital expenditure (CAPEX) creates assets that are subject to depreciation. Funding decisions may be difficult to change or reverse if priorities change. Operational expenditure (OPEX) is often the cost of normal business operations. Purchasing technology (for example) via OPEX and subscription services can allow an organisation to be more agile and flex when needed. However, any change will have some complexity associated with it, for example being 'locked in' to a particular vendor so that a move is difficult.

Figure 21 shows the 'fish model' (Lah and Wood, 2016) that defines the economies of subscription products and services. Revenue is generated in small, regular amounts rather than being loaded into an initial transaction. Initially, expenses increase as the organisation invests in its subscription offerings. Over time, revenues increase as customers are added in greater numbers, and expenses decrease. You'll probably have noticed that most software providers you work with have moved from annual licences or one-off fees to a subscription model.

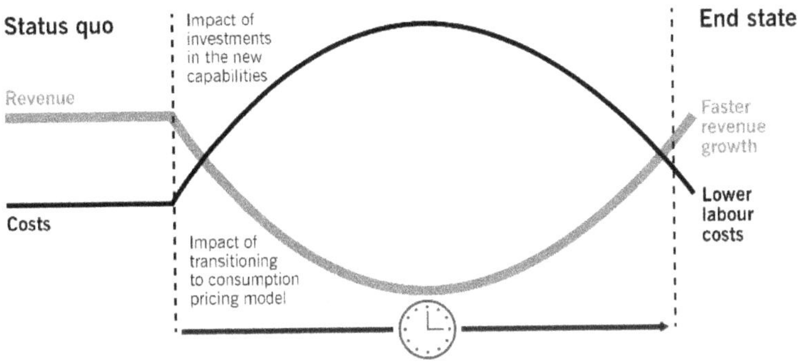

Figure 21: The fish model[26]

The move to subscription-based charging for software isn't just a financial decision. It's also a reflection of how we develop and maintain software, with ongoing updates and improvements as standard. Imagine if Microsoft had to post you a CD every time it updated its Office suite. Subscription access and Software-as-a-Service models allow software service providers to continually align to changing customer requirements and do smaller, less risky, more frequent updates.

---

[26] *ITIL® 4: Digital and IT Strategy*, Figure 5.2. From Lah, T. and Wood, J.B. (2016). Technology-as-a-Service Playbook: How to Grow a Profitable Subscription. ITIL® is a registered trade mark of the PeopleCert group. Used under licence from PeopleCert. All rights reserved.

Organisations can receive funding from:

- Investors
- Cash reserves
- Loans

Most digital products and services require significant investment before they are in a position to generate revenue, although Agile development can speed up time to market. An organisation needs to have sufficient funds for development, as well as funds to keep the organisation running during the development process, and funds to allow it to adapt to any changes. The funding mix (the sources of funding and how it will be allocated) is an important part of the financial element of a strategy.

The most common financial policies are based on one or more of the following:

- **Funding mix:** The availability of funding for strategic initiatives depends largely on the appetite of those who will be investing in the strategy, and their perspective on the strategic options.
- **Planning for growth:** Budgeting and funding practices must align to the level of agility or flexibility required by the strategy. These strategies use scenario planning and service models to show how spending will vary in different situations.
- **Tax-based strategies:** Large corporations may base their strategy on which countries provide the best tax advantages for each type of business activity.

Portfolio optimisation

A portfolio is *"a collection of assets into which an organization chooses to invest its resources in order to receive the best return"*.

Organisations use portfolios to track investments across the lifecycle of the associated products and services. The portfolio lens can help link an investment to the anticipated value proposition, making the portfolio a strategic tool to support effective decision-making about investments across new and existing products and services.

From a service management perspective, there are three main types of portfolio:

- **Product and service portfolio:** represents the commitments and investments by the service provider across customers and market spaces.
- **Programme and project portfolio:** used to manage and coordinate projects, this portfolio helps assure that deadlines are met and budget and scope are managed. It can also help reduce duplication between projects.
- **Customer portfolio:** this tracks commitments to customer groups and market spaces. It can influence the contents of the product and service portfolio, and helps visualise the relationship between business outcomes, customers, and products and services.

Organisations may also create portfolios to help the management of resources, applications, customer groups, business segments, etc. as required. It doesn't matter what is included in a portfolio – the key objective remains the same. Managing the portfolio should help deliver optimal return on investment from the assets tracked by the portfolio. Portfolio management tracks investment right through the lifecycle of an asset, product or service.

How good is your organisation at tracking return on investment for its new products and services? Many organisations that I've worked with have a very rigorous business case and approvals process, but once the money is committed very little effort is put into assessing whether it has been used well. This is a danger of 'traditional' funding models where the money is allocated and then can't be reallocated. In some of the public-sector organisations I've worked with, the money has to be spent or the overall budget will be decreased in the next financial year. This can even lead to projects being completed when really they should have been stopped partway through as they no longer align to business goals.

An advantage of Agile development is the focus on increments, including funding increments. If an organisation is working in a more Agile way, projects can be stopped if they will no longer deliver value before too much investment has been made.

Figure 22 shows how portfolio management helps achieve optimal ROI.[27]

[27] *ITIL® 4: Digital and IT Strategy*, Figure 5.13. ITIL® is a registered trade mark of the PeopleCert group. Used under licence from PeopleCert.

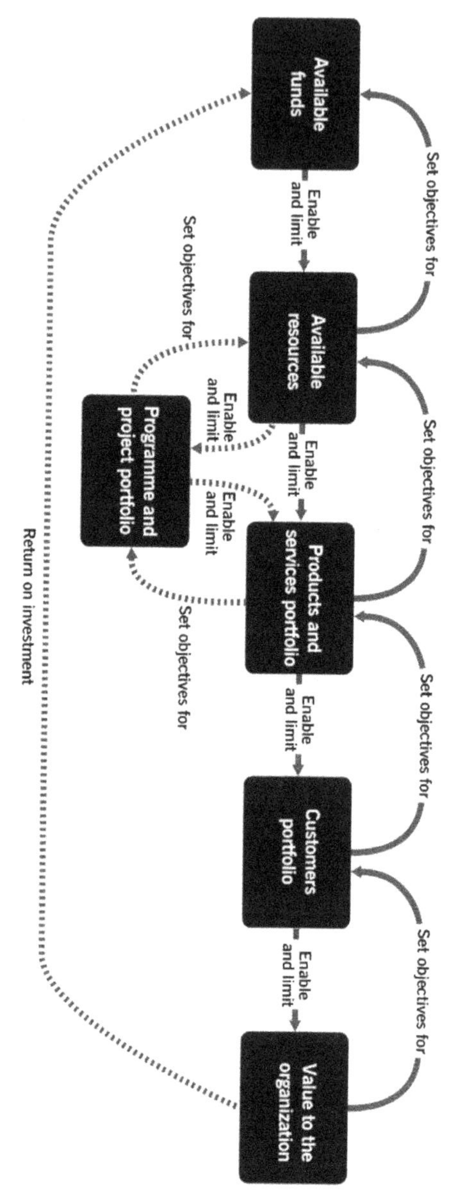

Figure 22: An organization's portfolios enable a return on investments

Funding projects, products and services

Most projects require some level of investment, even if they are not linked to strategic objectives. Projects such as hardware upgrades, or compliance work, will still need investment beyond the normal operating budget. These projects deliver improvements or allow products and services to be maintained without changing performance, processes or activities.

These types of investment will still need to sit within the scope and policies of the financial strategy.

Balancing the cost of innovation and operation

Most organisations separate innovation and operations. Staff may move between 'innovative' and 'operations' teams to add relevant skills when needed. This approach can, however, lead to 'innovation silos' that deliver limited improvements that don't deliver value right across the organisation.

For agile organisations, innovation is part of the culture and embedded in how the organisation works on a daily basis. Innovation is emphasised at all levels, for example in employee objectives, team goals and operational budgets.

How do you share innovative ideas in your organisation? What would you do if you had a bright idea? Is there a mechanism for you to share it? There are many different aspects to encouraging innovation.

First, culture. Some organisations have a negative culture where problems are accepted and complained about, with no one ever taking the initiative to improve things. Second, a mechanism to make suggestions is important and should be as easy as possible. Third, management action – if no innovative ideas are acted on, people will stop sharing them. Finally, reward and recognition – the UK's Royal Navy, for example, has a staff suggestion scheme that is open to all staff both service and civilian. Any suggestions that *"show marked efficiency or [...] contribute in signal degree to the improvement of the appliances of the naval or marine forces"* are eligible for a financial reward via the Herbert Lott Naval Trust Fund.

Some organisations operate a 'full cost recovery model' or working capital fund. This approach allows operating expenses to be recovered from internal and external customers, to encourage organisational units to operate as a business, This approach is self-sustaining and delivers several benefits:

- Improved cost transparency, allowing customers to pay for what they consume and understand how their activities drive costs.
- Better strategic investment planning, as the recovered costs can be used for upgrades and product and service investment, aligned to customer needs.
- Stable funding, removing the reliance on variable capital investment.

To successfully adopt a full cost recovery model, organisations need to be able to forecast demand effectively, automate reporting to support transparency and have sufficient contingency planning in place if anticipated revenue is not achieved.

Charging models

There are many different strategies that can be used to determine how products and services are priced. Products and services need to be priced competitively based on their market and their competition, supported by a cost model that tracks price, cost and profitability.

Pricing models may need to change over time. New products and services can have a premium price, but as competitors launch similar offerings, the price may need to reduce. Service providers need to have a level of flexibility and clear policies about profitability and margins.

Products and services that are offered to internal consumers can also be priced in different ways. Transparency is important to reduce waste and ensure internal IT costs are competitive when compared to external suppliers.

This table shows some of the potential digital charging models:

Table 17: Common digital charging models

Model	Description
Free	The product or service is free to use, but may be supported by other revenue such as advertising or in-application purchases.

Freemium	The product or service is free to use but may only offer basic or limited functionality, offering the consumer access to paid services that unlock more features.
Tiered	The consumer has a choice about what level of functionality/service they want to pay for, e.g. bronze, silver or gold.
Dynamic/variable	Prices change, often in response to supply and demand (e.g. Uber 'surge' pricing).

Practice: Service financial management

Purpose

The purpose of the service financial management practice is *"to support the organization's strategies and plans for service management by ensuring that the organization's financial resources and investments are being used effectively"*.

The practice ensures that an organisation's services have the correct level of funding, and supports decision making by providing reliable financial information. Activities include:

- Providing information about product and service costs across the lifecycle;
- Planning and managing product and service budgets; and

- Forecasting and measuring revenue related to products and services if charging is in place.

It's important to understand the scope of this practice and how it interacts with other practices. For example, service financial management doesn't make funding decisions, prioritise investments or distribute profits. These decisions are within the scope of other practices including strategy, risk and portfolio management.

Service financial management doesn't include financial management activities that aren't directly related to products and services. The practice will not, for example, make decisions about credit, loans and interest, and it won't have any involvement in investment analysis and decisions.

Roles

Many IT and ITSM professionals don't have specific financial management skills. Accountants and financial analysts may need to support the practice and its activities. A mixture of skills is required including traditional organisational financial management and an understanding of the financial aspects of digital products and services. Different organisations will adopt different approaches to getting the right mix of skills within service financial management, including:

- Putting financial professionals into digital teams;
- Putting digital professionals into finance teams;
- Having a dedicated finance team within the IT department; and
- Providing specialised training for product and service management staff.

In areas such as financial management and contract management, organisations often assign work to service management professionals with the expectation that they'll have the right skills. However, many don't, and their employer doesn't offer any training. For an organisation to achieve its goals (both strategic and financial), the workforce and talent management will need to assess what skills are required and how to access them. The traditional skillset of a service management professional may need updating to meet the needs of a digital organisation. If these skills are missing, the cost can be very high both in financial and performance terms. For example, a poorly worded contract can mean thousands of pounds spent in additional work fees.

Practice success factors

There are two PSFs defined for the service financial management practice:

- *"Ensuring that the organization's service financial management supports its overall strategy and stakeholder requirements*
- *Ensuring that reliable financial information is available as needed to support decision-making"*

Table 18 describes the PSFs in more detail:

Table 18: Service financial management practice success factors

PSF: Service financial management supports the overall strategy and stakeholders
To fulfil this PSF, the practice must have a defined approach to identify costs and provide the necessary detail to support budgeting and pricing. This will help meet the practice purpose – to improve the quality of decision making with reliable and accurate product and service financial information. Remember that service financial management (like any practice) is an overhead in terms of the resources it consumes. The practice must deliver greater benefit than the cost of maintaining the practice. The ITIL guiding principles can be applied to ensure the practice delivers benefits: • **Focus on value:** who are the stakeholders and what do they need? Don't do more than is needed. • Progress iteratively with feedback: develop and expand the practice iteratively, adding more as required rather than trying to build everything at once. • **Collaborate and promote visibility:** work across teams to ensure that financial data is accurate, timely and relevant, and promote the benefits of service financial management. • **Think and work holistically:** understand the entire cost of product and service provision, rather than focusing on individual elements.

- **Keep it simple and practical:** tailor reports to the people who are using them, and seek feedback to support improvement.
- Optimise and automate: reduce manual reporting as far as possible.

PSF: Financial information is available

Service financial management is a subset of the organisation's overall financial management capability. Its primary focus is to provide reliable information to stakeholders, not just to focus on compliance and control.

Service financial management is closely linked to practices that provide other management information, including knowledge management, service configuration management and IT asset management. It also provides data to support decision making in strategy, risk, capacity and performance, availability, service continuity, workforce and talent and supplier management.

Put simply, the practice can provide immense value by making the right financial information available to the right audience at the right time.

Practice: Portfolio management

Purpose

The purpose of the portfolio management practice is *"to ensure that the organization has the right mix of programs, projects, products, and services to execute the organization's strategy within its funding and resource constraints"*. The practice helps an organisation effectively allocate, deploy and manage resources.

A portfolio, as discussed earlier in this chapter, is defined as *"a collection of assets into which an organization chooses to invest its resources in order to receive the best return"*.

Portfolio management is closely linked to service financial management. It is focused on optimising the return on investment for products and services. Without supporting financial data, it's very challenging to assess this return on investment.

Practice success factors

There are two PSFs defined for the portfolio management practice:

- *"Ensuring sound investment decisions for programs, projects, products, and services within the organization's resource constraints*
- *Ensuring the continual monitoring, review, and optimization of the organization's portfolios"*

The table below describes the PSFs in more detail:

Table 19: Portfolio management practice success factors

PSF: Ensuring sound investment decisions
Portfolio management needs to continually prioritise and reprioritise how resources are allocated across products and services. The prioritisation approach should be communicated clearly to all stakeholders to ensure transparency.

Prioritisation is crucial for strategic alignment; high-priority initiatives would be at the front of the queue for resources. The practice provides feedback to and consumes information from other practices including service financial management.

Portfolios are communication tools for stakeholders. To be effective, they need to have an owner who will review and update the portfolio regularly. The resources that portfolio management draws on come from all four dimensions of service management:

- Organizations and people (experience, knowledge, leaders, etc.).
- Value streams and processes (frameworks and approaches, etc.).
- Information and technology (applications, hardware, etc.).
- Partners and suppliers (contracts, alliances, etc.).

PSF: Continual monitoring, review and optimization

Once an investment is made, it needs to be monitored to ensure that the expected value is achieved. An investment might fail to deliver, or it may deliver value but no longer be aligned with the organisation's strategy. Regular reviews as part of the portfolio management practice will:

- Ensure resources and investments are allocated to the right areas;
- Standardise how value realisation is tracked, assessed and validated; and

- Allow comparison across portfolio items by using templates.

Each organisation will measure value in different ways, depending on its strategic objectives. Measures can focus on function, performance, profit, customer satisfaction, reputation, etc.

Regular 'health' reports support portfolio optimisation so that action can be taken to deal with underperforming items. Interventions and corrections will be made to continually align the portfolio with the overall strategy, including retiring services where appropriate.

Strategic approaches for digital organisations

Earlier in this chapter we looked at the Barrett model, which describes organisational values and can be used to help set an organisation's strategic focus – you can see a reminder of the model in Figure 23[28]:

[28] *ITIL® 4: Digital and IT Strategy*, Figure 5.3. ITIL® is a registered trade mark of the PeopleCert group. Used under licence from PeopleCert.

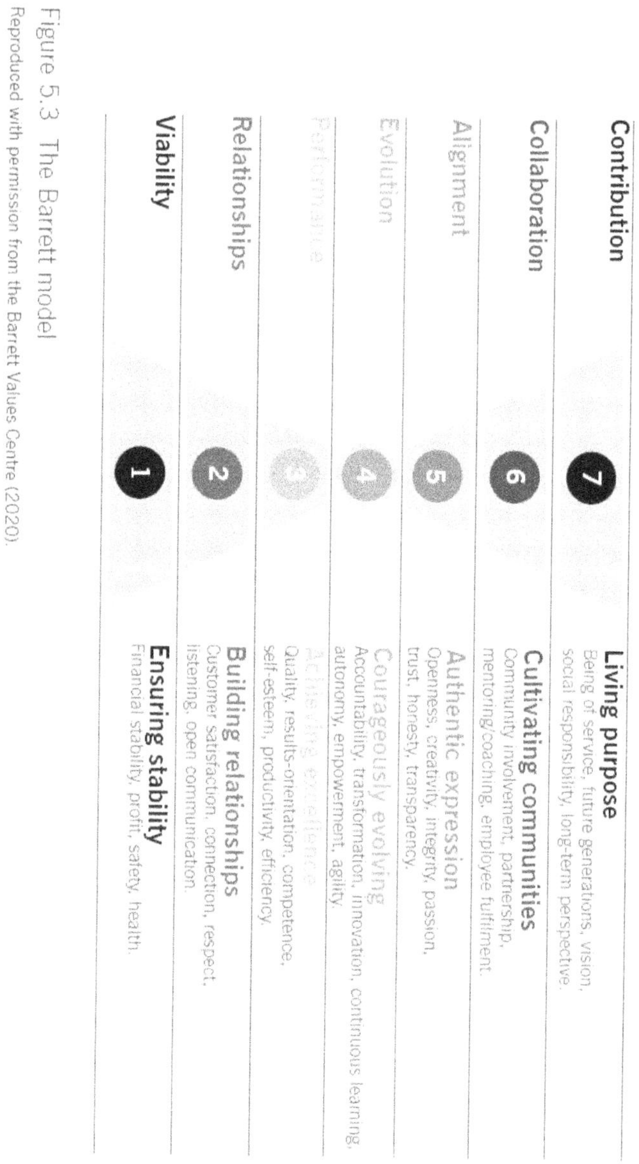

Contribution	7	**Living purpose** Being of service, future generations, vision, social responsibility, long-term perspective.
Collaboration	6	**Cultivating communities** Community involvement, partnership, mentoring/coaching, employee fulfilment.
Alignment	5	**Authentic expression** Openness, creativity, integrity, passion, trust, honesty, transparency.
Evolution	4	**Courageously evolving** Accountability, transformation, innovation, continuous learning, autonomy, empowerment, agility.
Performance	3	**Achieving excellence** Quality, results-orientation, competence, self-esteem, productivity, efficiency.
Relationships	2	**Building relationships** Customer satisfaction, connection, respect, listening, open communication.
Viability	1	**Ensuring stability** Financial stability, profit, safety, health.

Figure 5.3 The Barrett model

Reproduced with permission from the Barrett Values Centre (2020).

Figure 23: The Barrett model

An organisation can focus on:

- Foundational needs and values – levels 1–3;
- Evolution and transformation – level 4; and
- Purpose and contribution to common good – levels 5–7.

Organisations analyse internal and external factors as they decide on their strategic focus, allowing them to balance exploiting and protecting their current business model with the creation of a new one as required.

The table below shows how an organisation can group data into categories to support strategic decision making. The table gives some examples of where an organisation might change its business model or create a new one. The Barrett level of an organisation is significant in this decision-making process. Organisations at the higher levels are able to understand and react to changes at all levels – organisations at lower levels may struggle to understand and respond to changes at the higher levels. For example, an organisation that is focused on level 1 and remaining profitable may miss market signals about a new focus on social responsibility that its competitors exploit to gain market advantage.

Table 20: Information that supports business model planning[29]

Key values according to the Barrett model	***Signs suggesting that the business model is being***	***Signs suggesting a need to protect or review the business model***

[29] *ITIL® 4: Digital and IT Strategy*, Table 5.3. ITIL® is a registered trade mark of the PeopleCert group. Used under licence from PeopleCert.

	exploited or should evolve	
Purpose (alignment / collaboration / contribution)	• *New needs of society* • *New opportunities for collaboration and value co-creation*	• *New regulations challenging the business model* • *Feedback indicating a decline in the value perceived by the stakeholders*
Evolution (transformation)	• *Other external factors suggesting a need or opportunity to transform the business* • *Innovative ideas being generated in the organization, suggesting a transformation opportunity*	• *External opportunities that cannot be used within the current business model* • *Large-scale disasters affecting the relevance and viability of the current business model and strategy*

5: Approaches to achieve market relevance and operational excellence

Foundation (viability / relationships / performance)	• *Opportunity or a new business model due to new or emerging technology* • *Removal of a barrier to entry for customers who were excluded from the existing market, by providing cheaper prices or simpler solutions*	• *A declining trend in performance metrics such as market value, customer retention, product or service sales, or customer satisfaction* • *Difficulty in finding new ways to enhance offerings and value propositions for the current business model*

Strategic approaches to evolution

To adapt and take advantage of emerging opportunities, organisations need to be open to change and evolution. We're going to look at a range of different strategic approaches in this section that can help organisations evolve successfully. These include:

- Innovation;
- Agility and resilience;

- Organisational change management;
- Knowledge management;
- Social responsibility and sustainability;
- Triple bottom line; and
- Employee fulfilment.

We'll cover the key content that is required by the syllabus (as well as a few stories along the way), but why not make a note of the approaches you find the most interesting? You can investigate them further once you have completed your studies and start to think about their relevance for your current organisation and where you could make positive changes.

Strategic approaches: innovation

Innovation is defined in the ITIL® 4: Digital and IT Strategy publication as *"adoption of a novel technology or way of working that has led to the significant improvement of an organization, product, or service"*.

New technology and new ways of working don't guarantee that innovation will occur. True innovation may use technology but it must also increase or improve value delivered.

It may be necessary to create a value stream for innovations, which will involve practices including:

- Business analysis;
- Portfolio management;
- Project management;
- Change enablement;
- Organisational change management;

- Workforce and talent management; and
- Relationship management.

This approach will ensure that the organisation doesn't have an 'innovation silo'. Innovation may come from any area of the organisation and needs to be embedded appropriately if it is to be effective as a strategic approach.

Any innovation initiatives that are identified should be acted on quickly. It's a good idea to involve the initiators or at a minimum provide a level of transparency so that the initiator knows what is happening. Feedback loops provide information on success/failure, and failure should be 'allowed' within the corporate culture. Innovation cannot thrive in an organisation where people are scared to fail.

Strategic approaches: agility and resilience

We looked at the definitions of organisational agility and resilience earlier in this book. As a reminder, organisational agility is *"an organization's ability of to move and adapt quickly, flexibly, and decisively in response to events in the internal or external environment"*, and organisational resilience is *"an organization's ability to anticipate, prepare for, respond to, and overcome adverse events in the internal or external environment"*.

PESTLE analysis can be used to understand the external influences that will affect the organisation.

Using the information in the case study and your own knowledge, carry out a PESTLE analysis for Banksbest. Are there any high-priority or high-impact factors that Banksbest needs to focus on as part of its strategic planning?

Strategic approaches: organisational change management

How often have you seen organisational change management (OCM) done well? I can probably count on one hand the number of times I've seen really effective OCM in place. One global client of mine has an OCM team consisting of one person, who is hopelessly overworked. OCM is an essential component of every change that we make and so is arguably one of the most critical organisational practices.

An example of this comes via the Scopism Global SIAM Survey. Every year, organisations from all over the world provide information about their experience with service integration and management (SIAM). One of the questions asks about the challenges that they faced adopting SIAM. Since 2018, OCM and embedding new behaviours has

> always been the biggest challenge. No matter what we're doing, OCM will be key.

Whatever type of change is planned, we must take people along with us – and that requires a concerted effort. OCM can reduce the risks associated with a change and reduce any negative impact on products, services and the customer experience. Any organisation that wishes to make changes successfully should:

- Develop and nurture a culture that enables change to take place;
- Have a holistic approach to OCM and continually measure and improve OCM performance; and
- Actively work to ensure that changes are effective, and that they meet stakeholder and compliance requirements.

ITIL® 4 suggests some OCM principles:

- Have clear, relevant objectives.
- Have strong and committed leadership.
- Focus on sustained improvement.
- Create willing, prepared participants.

It's a good idea to read the ITIL® 4 organizational change management practice guide for more detail about this practice.

Strategic approaches: knowledge management

An evolving organisation needs to be a learning organisation. If an organisation and its people are 'closed' to new ideas, it will be very hard to generate any innovation or improvement. An organisation should have a strategy for both continual professional development and knowledge management.

The absorptive capacity of an organisation is defined as *"an organization's ability to recognize the value of new information, embed it into an existing knowledge system, and apply it to achieve the intended business outcomes"*. Absorptive capacity can be increased by creating and using new knowledge within the organisation, drawing on internal and external sources.

The figure below shows the SECI model.

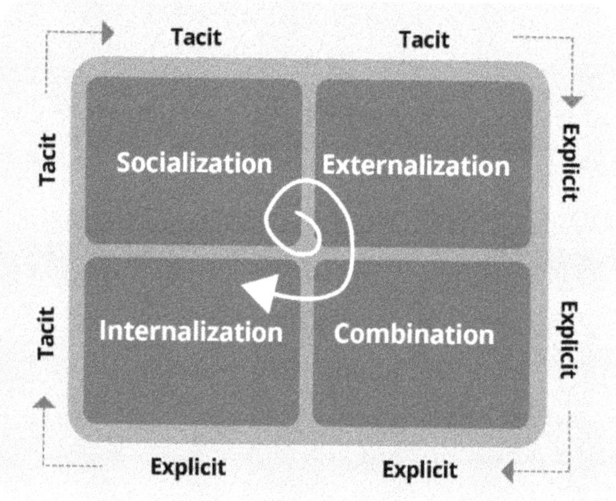

Figure 24: The development of knowledge-sharing according to the SECI model - (Nonaka & Takeuchi, 1995)[30]

---

[30] *ITIL® 4: Digital and IT Strategy*, Figure 5.10. ITIL® is a registered trade mark of the PeopleCert group. Used under licence from PeopleCert.

The model describes explicit and tacit knowledge:

- **Explicit knowledge** – transferrable to others, codified, assessed, verbalised, stored (for example, books, databases, descriptions, etc.).
- **Tacit knowledge** – this is more difficult to transfer to others, to codify, or to express; it is based on experience, values, capabilities, skills.

The model is based on the ability to convert tacit to explicit knowledge as well as to transfer it from an individual to a group. The quadrants and possible transfers of knowledge include the following:

- **Socialisation (tacit to tacit)** – sharing knowledge face-to-face or through experiences, such as coaching, meetings, and so on.
- **Externalisation (tacit to explicit)** – describing the experience or formulating the process/guidelines.
- **Combination (explicit to explicit)** – combining, analysing and presenting data from inside and outside an organisation to form new knowledge.
- **Internalisation (explicit to tacit)** – an individual develops their knowledge independently or through formal training.

Knowledge should be transformed into reusable knowledge assets that can be shared and used across the organisation to support decision making.

Technology is changing the world of work, but there are other changes taking place as well. Knowledge workers may move to new organisations and will need to take charge of their own learning and development rather than expecting their employer to manage this.

If your organisation isn't great at developing you, you need to take charge of your own development. I've been in service management for more than 20 years and there's always something new to learn. It can be overwhelming at times, but it's so important to keep hold of your curiosity and not be closed off to new ideas.

Take charge of your personal development with whatever time and resources are available. If you can persuade your manager to support you in the idea, why not introduce learning time across your team? I've worked with organisations that have a set budget per employee per year that is for them to learn something new; this can be anything from attending a conference to buying a robot.

If you don't get any support at work, do what you can. Listen to a podcast on your commute or at the gym, read an article while you're stood in a line…the Internet has opened up a world of new ideas. As you advance, look for ways to contribute as well as to consume. Are there any communities you can get involved with?

Strategic approaches: social responsibility and sustainability

Sustainability is defined as a *"business approach focused on creating long-term value for society and other stakeholders by addressing the risks and opportunities associated with economic, environmental, and social developments"*. This definition has evolved from the original, more narrow meaning that was focused on environmental factors only. It now includes employee fulfilment and their need for purpose, expressed via the triple bottom line (we'll cover both of these in the following sections).

Social responsibility and sustainability aren't just 'nice' ideas – these concepts are being recognised globally at the most senior levels. There is a new acceptance that organisations exist to do more than just create money for shareholders.

For example, the bosses of 181 of the US's biggest companies have changed the official definition of "the purpose of a corporation" from making the most money possible for shareholders to *"improving our society"* by also looking out for employees, caring for the environment and dealing ethically.

Big business bosses signing up to the change include Jeff Bezos, the founder and chief executive of Amazon; the

Apple boss, Tim Cook; and Jamie Dimon, chairman and CEO of Wall Street bank JPMorgan.[31]

The UK's Corporate Governance Code (2018) states this in its introduction: *"Companies do not exist in isolation. Successful and sustainable businesses underpin our economy and society by providing employment and creating prosperity. To succeed in the long-term, directors and the companies they lead need to build and maintain successful relationships with a wide range of stakeholders."*

Strategic approaches: triple bottom line

Figure 25 shows the three focus areas of the triple bottom line approach.[32]

[31] Source: https://www.theguardian.com/business/2019/aug/19/leading-us-bosses-group-drops-principle-of-shareholder-first.

[32] *ITIL® 4: Digital and IT Strategy*, Figure 5.11. ITIL® is a registered trade mark of the PeopleCert group. Used under licence from PeopleCert. All rights reserved.

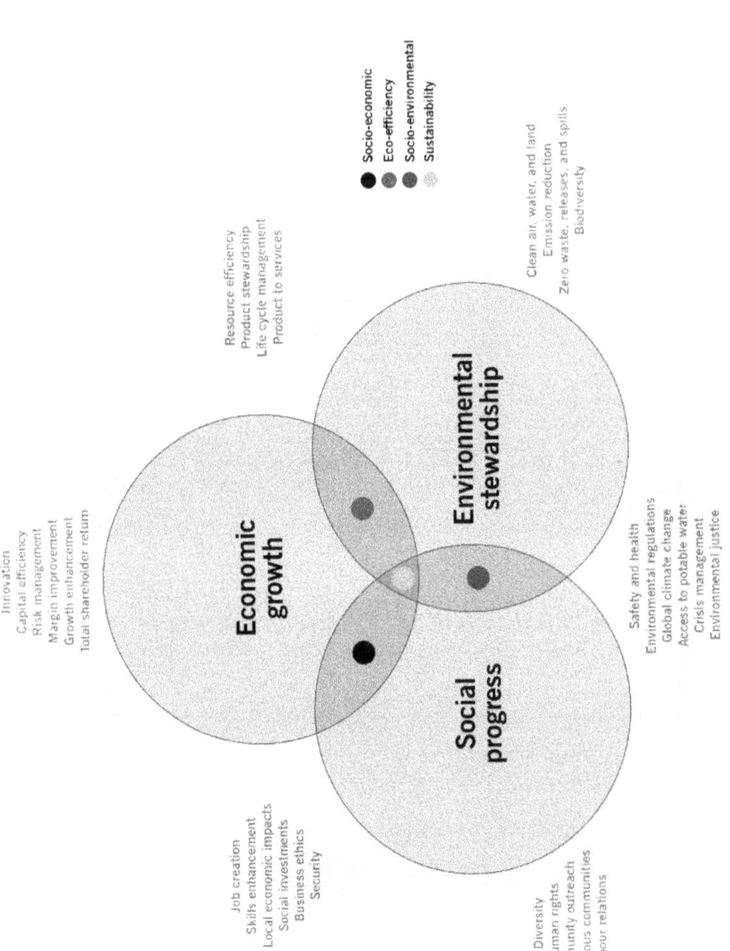

Figure 25: The triple bottom line model

Organisations that adopt this approach focus on more than just profitability; they are focused on economic, social and environmental factors. This requires them to adopt sustainability (in the broadest sense) as a strategic initiative. Sustainability needs to be embedded in all teams, value streams, products and services.

An organisation adopting the triple bottom line will need clear policies that are embedded in practices including architecture management, supplier management, business analysis, relationship management, service design and portfolio management. The practices will then, in turn, provide inputs into strategy definition.

Strategic approach: employee fulfilment

Is an employee an asset or a liability? What do employees want from their work, beyond financial recompense for their time?

Employee fulfilment positions employees as stakeholders, with needs that must be understood and met. Many employees are now looking for work that gives them a sense of purpose, in addition to job satisfaction, rewards, etc. This shift can be seen in the language used in many organisations, moving from 'human resources' to 'workforce and talent management'. Employee acquisition is expensive, so organisations can see financial benefits if they can acquire and retain the right talent.

Employee fulfilment is defined as the *"feeling that people have when their work aligns with their intrinsic motivation and provides them with a sense of purpose"*. Organisations need to provide opportunities that emphasise relationships, impact and growth. This can be expressed through:

- Meaningful work relationships;
- How contributions are viewed; and
- Development based on overcoming personal challenges.

So, what's stopping every organisation from focusing on employee fulfilment? Possible obstacles can be found at every level – leadership, management, team members and employees themselves. Organisational culture must change to support this approach. You can read more about this in the ITIL® 4 workforce and talent management practice guide.

Figure 26 shows the evolution of work – you will notice the correlation between this and the Barrett model that we studied earlier. Organisations that don't provide meaning and fulfilment to their employees risk losing them, or receiving sub-standard work.[33]

[33] *ITIL® 4: Digital and IT Strategy*, Figure 5.12. ITIL® is a registered trade mark of the PeopleCert group. Used under licence from PeopleCert. All rights reserved.

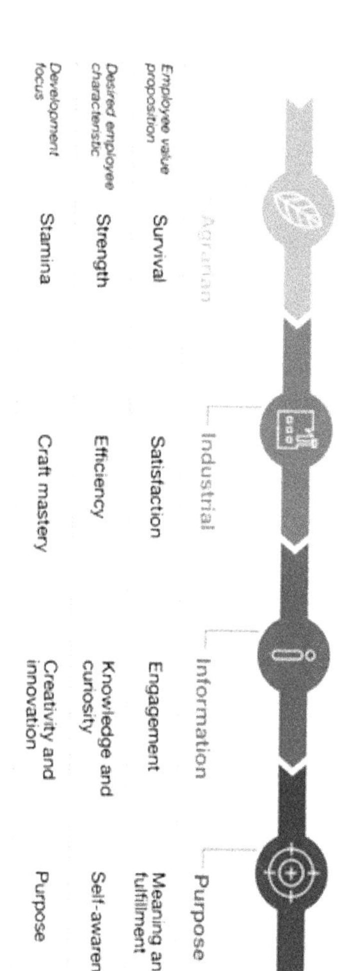

Figure 26: Evolution of work

CHAPTER 6: DIGITAL AND IT STRATEGY OPPORTUNITIES AND RISKS

In this chapter, we'll look at the risks associated with Digital and IT Strategy and also the opportunities for innovation. This chapter includes:

- Risk management in a digital organisation;
- How to identify and assess risk;
- Risk posture, and how to balance risk and opportunity;
- Key elements and techniques for innovation; and
- Techniques for developing and maintaining an innovation culture.

Risk management for digital organisations

Digital organisations have access to great opportunities, but must also manage the possibility of disruption and the risks associated with it. Digital transformation initiatives can safeguard an organisation's future, or they can waste huge amounts of money and not deliver results. Effective risk management is needed to make sure that benefits are maximised and risks are understood and mitigated where necessary. This happens at different levels of the organisation:

- Strategic risk management focuses on success in an environment where digital technology has changed the accepted ways of doing things.
- Tactical risk management focuses on identifying ways to address individual threats and vulnerabilities, both new and existing.

Risk is defined as *"a possible event that could cause harm or loss, or make it more difficult to achieve objectives"*. It can also be defined as uncertainty of outcome, when an action may generate positive or negative results but the picture isn't clear. Negative outcomes lead to harm or loss, and positive risk can lead to the exploitation of opportunities.

The risk management practice aims to ensure that an organisation understands risks and addresses them effectively. Risk management activities will typically include:

- *"conducting environmental analyses to identify and frame risks*
- *determining and documenting the organization's risk capacity and risk appetite*
- *documenting risk management policies*
- *identifying, analysing, and evaluating risks*
- *determining the appropriate risk treatment*
- *identifying risk triggers and owners*
- *ensuring risk strategies are implemented appropriately".*

In a digital organisation, the risk management approach will be affected by the overall transformation approach, as shown in the table below.

Table 21: Transformation approaches and risk management

Transformation approach	Risk management approach
Process-based paradigm	The risk management approach will follow a process, for example assess current state, define target future

	state, identify risks associated with the change.
Model-based paradigm	Risk management would be involved in the identification of different business cases for possible models and assessing the risks associated with each one.

Digital organisations have many opportunities, but they need to manage the risks associated with them. Looking at the Banksbest case study, what risks are associated with the organisation's strategic goals? Can they be mitigated in any way?

Digital technology exposes an organisation to risk at every level. Cyber security risks, for example, can affect the entire organisation (a hack, or a failed business venture) or a single individual (a virus or a lost piece of hardware). The digital assets that an organisation relies on are everywhere – they can't be controlled by locking the door of the server room. Everyone in the organisation needs to be aware of risk management and the role that they have to play.

By their very nature, digital organisations are innovative, flexible and open to change. They cannot exist in a risk-free environment. Instead, they need to focus on taking small, calculated risks in a managed way.

The ultimate accountability for risk management sits with the governing body of the organisation. It can't be outsourced or delegated. Executives must implement an appropriate risk management framework, and monitor its execution and performance. Every organisation should have a risk management practice, established in line with the organisation's overall appetite for risk. The practice is usually maintained by a risk or audit committee, while specialists such as the CISO will implement risk measures.

Risk identification

Most frameworks (including some we've already studied) include risk management and risk categories. The table below shows some examples:

Table 22: Risk prompts and frameworks

Framework	Details
PESTLE	To support scanning the business environment, Francis J. Aguilar (1967) proposed 'ETPS' to describe four sectors of taxonomy of the environment: Economic, Technical, Political and Social.
VUCA	Developed by Bennis and Nanus to support appropriate responses to different conditions and situations.
TECOP	Risk prompts focused on the internal environment. TECOP stands for technical, economic, cultural, organisational, political.

OODA	A recurring decision-making cycle created by the US Air Force, OODA stands for observe-orient-decide-act.
Porter's five forces	Can be used to assess competitive threats to an organisation.
Force-field analysis	An approach from social sciences, it assesses the positive and negative factors associated with a change.

One approach to risk identification that is particularly relevant to the digital world is DICE – disruption, innovation, cyber security and engagement. The table below explains DICE in more detail.

Table 23: DICE

Disruption risks	These risks threaten an organisation's business model. They can be a result of new digital technology (for example, the Cloud) or can affect how technology is used (for example, new legislation). Disruption risks can provide competitive advantage and are particularly significant in industries that are slow to change, leaving the incumbent organisation(s) at risk of new entrants. Consumers may also provide disruption by demanding new products and services, or ways to access existing products and services. There is also the ever-present risk of new

	technology being adopted and not living up to its promises.
Innovation risks	Innovation risks often come from the need to balance speed to market with effective products and services. Launch something of poor quality, and business reputation may be affected. Innovation may not deliver the expected results, and can lead to an 'arms race' where organisations continually chase their competition to try to catch up.
Cyber security risks	Cyber security risks increase as organisations become more digital. Risks can exist inside and outside the organisation, and the loss of data can have both financial and reputational consequences. The increase in cyber security risks has led to innovation in this market, with specialist services offered by threat intelligence vendors.
Engagement risks	Engagement risks occur across a range of different stakeholders, for example: • **Consumers** – can easily switch to a new supplier in the digital world. • **Suppliers** – may not be able to provide the services the organisation needs. • **Regulatory bodies** – may prevent an organisation from exploiting a new

	opportunity (for example, legislation to stop e-scooters in some cities).

Risk assessment and treatment

So, how does an organisation successfully understand risks and apply an appropriate response? One way to achieve this is to adopt a mixture of qualitative and quantitative risk assessment techniques.

Qualitative risk assessment determines the likelihood of a risk occurring and the impact it will have. This allows risks to be prioritised. Figure 27 shows a typical risk matrix.

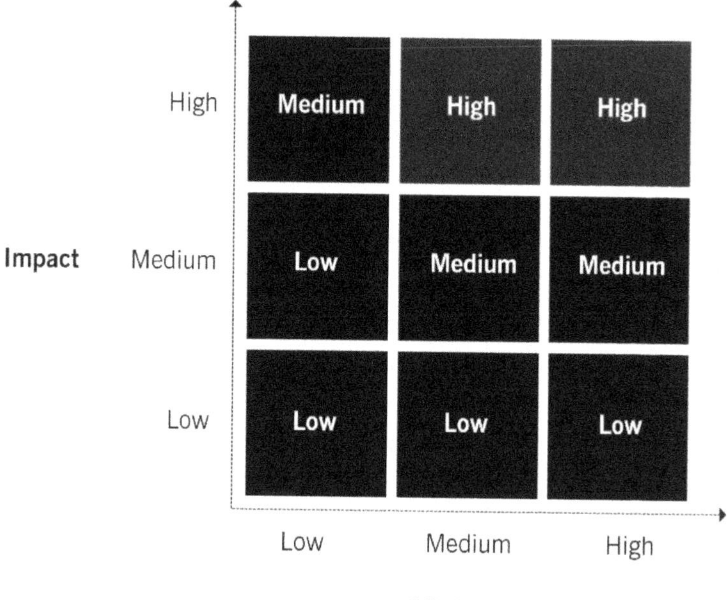

Figure 27: Matrix example for qualitative risk analysis[34]

Using the matrix, an organisation can map risk impact against risk likelihood. High risks will typically need to be eliminated. Medium risks may be mitigated and low risks may be accepted with no action taken (although they still need to be recorded and monitored in case the situation changes).

Organisations can also use scenario-based assessment as part of qualitative risk assessment. This follows a process that allows organisations to evaluate opportunities and decide

[34] *ITIL® 4: Digital and IT Strategy*, Figure 11.1. ITIL® is a registered trade mark of the PeopleCert group. Used under licence from PeopleCert.

whether to exploit them based on the associated positive and negative risks. Scenario-based assessment includes:

- Describing the opportunity (for example, using a business model canvas);
- Listing any assumptions or incomplete data;
- Identifying any variables;
- Projecting the effects of challenging assumptions or changing variables;
- Assessing the impact of each change and its likelihood; and
- Identifying actions to remove or reduce negative risks and to increase the likelihood of the positive risks.

Lucy Jones, the product owner for My Way at Banksbest, has been asked to carry out some scenario analysis for her project. She has been asked to consider:

- Good publicity for the services leading to demand from clients outside the UK and the possibility of a new international banking service; and
- The potential to add non-banking services such as insurance.

Carry out scenario analysis for both of these options. Should Banksbest move forward with either scenario?

Quantitative risk assessment attempts to put a financial value on risks. This is a more complex approach and may involve significant costs, including research and analysis. Because of the associated costs, quantitative analysis may only be applied to higher-level risks, in line with the organisation's overall risk appetite. Some of the calculations that are used include the following:

- **Annual rate of occurrence (ARO):** what is the probability that the risk will occur in a given year?
- **Single loss expectancy (SLE):** what is the expected financial loss related to the risk, each time it occurs?
- **Annualised loss expectancy (ALE):** what is the expected financial loss when averaged over a year? This can be calculated by multiplying the SLE by the ARO.

Risk posture

Risk posture is defined as *"an organization's overall approach to identifying, analyzing, planning for, responding to, and managing risk"*. It can be analysed by looking at an organisation's risk appetite (the overall risk an organisation can accept in aggregate) and risk tolerance (the risk an organisation can accept per individual risk). An organisation must understand how much risk it will accept to develop a strategy to address risk management. 'Risk capacity' is sometimes used as a term to express how much total risk an organisation will tolerate.

Each organisation will develop its own risk attitude, defined as a *"typical response to risk, based on risk capacity, appetite, tolerance, and thresholds"*.

Table 24 shows some common classifications for risk attitude. Bear in mind that an organisation's position may change over time and as its market, products and services evolve.

Table 24: Attitudes to risk

Risk attitude	Detail
Risk-averse	This type of organisation or individual will overestimate negative and underestimate positive risks. They're unlikely to adopt a strategy that requires significant change and may not pursue disruptive, digital opportunities. They will only change when they are forced to, and when other organisations have already led the way.
Risk-seeking	This type of organisation or individual will underestimate negative risks and overestimate positive risks. They may rush into new areas without fully understanding what could go wrong, so they need a strategy that will allow them to manage the different outcomes they could experience. Many startups will be in this category; there are huge opportunities, but the associated risk is high.
Risk-tolerant	This type of organisation or individual is content with the status quo and will not seek to make radical changes. They are comfortable with their existing level of negative risk and not pursuing any actions that involve positive risk. This in itself can be a risky attitude if their market or sector is evolving around them.

Risk-neutral	This type of organisation or individual has a long-term approach to risk. Positive and negative risks are assessed in the context of the digital and IT strategy, giving a healthy attitude to risk that is encouraged at all levels of the organisation. Input from stakeholders who are risk-averse and risk-seeking provides an overall balanced approach.

Risk treatment or mitigation

Risk treatment or risk mitigation refers to the collective policies, plans, processes and tools that an organisation uses to manage risk. This includes identifying, assessing and mitigating risks where necessary. The table below shows some of the common categories of risk treatment:

Table 25: Risk treatments

Risk treatment category	Details
Risk retention/acceptance	The impact and/or probability of the risk is less than the investment that would be required to prevent it, so the organisation decides to take no action. The risk will still be monitored.
Risk avoidance	A risk probability is very high or the risk would be too expensive to mitigate, so the organisation decides not to

	pursue the action that would lead to the risk arising.
Risk-sharing/transfer	The organisation invests in a partnership where the partner can take some (or all) of the risk, for example by moving from its own data centre to a Cloud hosting provider. The risk can be transferred, but the original organisation still bears the accountability for it.
Risk modification/reduction	The organisation acts to reduce the impact or probability of the risk, for example by using role-based access control to reduce security risks, or hardware redundancy to reduce the risk of failure.

Risk-informed culture

An organisation's executive is responsible for determining its risk posture and attitude. They can create (or not!) a risk-informed mindset and culture that encourages everyone in the organisation to see themselves as part of the overall risk management efforts.

Risk management and an effective risk culture are closely linked to psychological safety within an organisation. I've worked with several businesses where I can see that people feel it's safer just to 'keep quiet' rather than flag a risk and draw attention to something that they might be blamed for. Think about this in the context of your own employer, or organisations that you've recently worked with. If you became aware of a risk, how would you raise it? What action would be taken? Would you feel safe?

Risk aware is not the same as risk averse. An organisation that practises effective risk management will get better, and faster, at identifying risks and taking the appropriate action, allowing them to exploit opportunities and manage negative risks.

Digital organisations should:

- Reward risk-taking within boundaries – allowing employees to fail fast, learn and experiment;
- Identify and reduce recklessness; and
- Carry out ongoing education, communication and awareness.

Practice: Risk management

Purpose

The purpose of the risk management practice is *"to ensure that the organization understands and effectively handles risks"*. Almost every service is a balance between adding risk to the consumer and removing risk from the consumer. For example, online banking removes risks associated with carrying cash, manual transactions, etc., but adds risks such as online fraud and identity theft. The risk management practice allows an organisation to identify and manage risks across all four dimensions of service management.

There are three levels of risk management defined in the ITIL® 4 risk management practice guide:

- **Strategic:** associated with long-term risks that could affect strategic goals.
- **Program and project:** associated with mid-term, project and programme goals and objectives.
- **Operational:** associated with short-term goals and objectives.

Practice success factors

There are four practice success factors for the risk management practice:

- *"Establishing governance of risk management*
- *Nurturing a risk management culture and identifying risks*
- *Analyzing and evaluating risks*
- *Treating, monitoring, and reviewing risks"*

Table 26: Risk management practice success factors

PSF: Establish governance
To effectively govern risk, the practice (and the organisation) needs to understand two concepts: • **Risk capacity** – *"The maximum amount of risk an organization can tolerate (typically based on damage to reputation, assets, etc.)"* • **Risk appetite** – *"The amount of risk the organization is willing to accept (should always be less than the risk capacity)"* These will be defined via organisational governance, which provides boundaries for how an organisation operates. Risk management should be discussed regularly at board meetings, including a review of risk governance, risk capacity, risk appetite and any strategic risks.
PSF: Nurture a risk management culture
A risk management culture needs to be open and honest. It isn't always easy to identify a risk and employees may be frightened to highlight a risk if they think they will be blamed. It must be seen as everyone's responsibility to identify and report risks; some organisations may need to allow anonymous reports while they address their risk management culture. As with any element of organisational culture, risk management culture needs to be assessed for effectiveness and regularly nurtured. Risks that have been identified need to be recorded in a risk register, which records the risk and other information including status and history.

PSF: Analyse and evaluate risks
Earlier in this chapter we looked at qualitative risk analysis based on impact and likelihood, and then quantitative analysis based on financial or numerical impact. An organisation should use both types of risk analysis to build a balanced approach in a resource-effective way.
PSF: Treat, monitor and review risks
As part of its risk management activities, an organisation needs to document accepted risks, communicate with stakeholders, and regularly review risks for any changes in probability, impact, or the cost of controls. When a risk is accepted, the organisation will design and implement agreed controls to mitigate or overcome the risk. All controls should be regularly reviewed for compliance, and action is taken if the control isn't being followed. Controls will apply to all four dimensions of service management.

Encouraging and managing innovation

So far in this chapter we've discussed risk and risk management – now, we turn our attention to innovation. Innovation and risk often go together, and it is here that the 'positive' outcomes related to a risk can happen. We're going to look at:

- Innovation as a strategic capability;
- Innovation as a mindset and culture;
- A balanced approach to innovation;

- Innovation management;
- Building an innovation-supporting culture; and
- Approaches to innovation.

Innovation is a key part of a digital organisation. Most digital organisations are disruptive by nature, but even those with more limited goals must be able to adapt to the continual changes in technology and ways of working. Innovation does not just make new capabilities and efficiencies available to organisations, but can change the nature of their internal and external environments. To be successful, a digital organisation needs to be able, at a minimum, to track, adopt and adapt innovations that will allow them to maintain or protect their position.

Innovation can be:

- Large and transformational or small and incremental;
- Applied to products, services, structure or supply chains; and
- Applied internally or to the customer experience.

Innovation is defined within ITIL® 4 as the *"adoption of a novel technology or way of working that has led to the significant improvement of an organization, product, or service"*. Innovation only takes place in this definition when something is adopted and change is created. The fact that something exists isn't innovative; innovation only happens when something is used. Discontinuous innovation is *"an innovation that completely replaces what came before"*.

Organisations need to track changes that are happening around them and identify where innovation may be possible. They need to focus on both continual improvement analysis and effective implementation of selected technologies, ways of working, etc. As we mentioned in earlier chapters, this may require an innovation value stream, but the team working on this value stream must not exist in a silo.

Innovation as a strategic capability

It's often said that history is written by the winners. Many of the business stories we are told that relate to innovation are from the organisations that did succeed. It's tempting for other organisations to copy the stories, without the context that led to the success in the first place. The stories of organisations that got things wrong can be as interesting and as educational as those that succeed, but these stories are also harder to find.

There is no quick fix and no 'five steps to easy innovation'. Organisations need to see innovation as a strategic capability; a muscle that needs to be exercised and built up over time. Managing innovation actively can help an organisation succeed in a volatile environment. Remember that innovation may be applied to:

- Determine the organisation's strategic position;
- Improve performance and competitive position; and
- Challenge existing strategies and objectives.

Digital leadership uses innovation deliberately, choosing what will best help the organisation meet its strategic goals. Not every innovation is necessary or valuable for every organisation.

I'd sum up this section of the book by saying that 'you can't copy culture'. If you go to IT events or listen to industry webinars, you'll hear people talking about Spotify or Zappos as examples of innovative organisations that they are using for inspiration. Zappos is often cited as an innovation example because of the 'holacracy' structure it adopted, creating a flat system with no managers, no job titles and no hierarchy. Sounds great! But did it work? Not entirely. Many staff left, and the absence of formal job titles and roles created a vacuum that could be filled informally. Gradually, Zappos has backed away from holacracy, but this doesn't stop it being a great headline or slide filler in many presentations.[35] Commoditised services are easy to copy. Culture? Not so much.

Innovation is a mindset and a culture

Innovation only adds value when it solves a problem – innovation for innovation's sake is not adding value. Many industry-changing ideas come from entrepreneurs and startups, as well as from well-funded research and development teams in larger organisations. Entrepreneurs and startups are often successful because they are very close to their customer and customer needs; they have to be aligned

---

[35] This is a fascinating overview of the Zappos story: *https://www.bbc.co.uk/programmes/m000t48x*

with their customer to have the funds to continue to operate. Innovation is the result of trying to solve a problem, not a goal to aim towards.

You've been invited to work with Banksbest as a consultant to help them build a more innovative culture. The executives are concerned that innovation opportunities are being missed, for example because staff in the branches don't have any mechanism to share ideas. What would you recommend they do to support innovation?

Balanced approach to innovation

Innovation can have rewards, but is also by its nature risky and potentially disruptive. Uncontrolled innovation that isn't linked to overall strategic goals can be chaotic and wasteful. Managing innovation requires managing uncertainty; in a situation where we may not know the costs, the returns, if something will work, or if it will be accepted. It can be helpful for an organisation to develop an 'innovation posture' (similar to a risk posture) that will define tolerances for the following:

- **The overall innovation driver** – does the organisation HAVE to innovate, or is it currently 'nice to have'?
- **Ability to tolerate disruption** – how much uncertainty can the organisation handle?

- **Innovation intensity** – how much? How often? How transformative should innovation be?
- **Strategic alignment** – what if an innovation deviates from the current strategy?
- **Return on investment** – the expected minimum level.
- **Leverage** – the ratio between the size of the innovation and the outcome achieved.
- **Risk appetite** – as discussed in earlier sections.
- **Incentives to innovate** – are stakeholders motivated to innovate?

Innovation management

Managing innovation sounds like an oxymoron. How do we manage what we can't measure or anticipate? Organisations can manage innovation, but they need to develop a structure that balances formality with flexibility, allowing for the uncertainty and risk that comes with developing innovative products and services.

This could be in the form of an innovation management team, or it could be a smaller part of existing roles in an organisation. Even when an innovation management team is in place, it will be the subject matter experts and front-line staff from across the organisation who are doing the 'innovating'. Innovation management teams will report to the senior executive to maintain strategic alignment, and will support managers and teams who are the source of potential innovation.

The activities required to manage innovation include:

- Building a collective process with a shared sense of purpose;

- Creating a climate of collaboration and open communication, based on psychological safety principles; and
- Being able to capture and evaluate ideas quickly to deliver optimal results and identify where to invest.

Innovation management could follow these steps to allow ideas to progress (or not) in an efficient way:

- **Generate and capture ideas** – for example, using brainstorms, design thinking, innovation fairs, hackathons, etc.
- **Filter ideas** – will it 'help' the customer? Is it needed?
- **Incubate ideas** – move an idea from a concept to reality.
- **Evaluate ideas** – use established criteria (costs, return, business need, and so on) to accept or reject the idea (executives should set the criteria as well as evaluate).
- **Select ideas** – base selection evaluation ranking and potential to address challenge.
- **Identify/charter a team to build/test** – roles could include the proposer, technical experts, architects, project management, organisational component experts.
- **Develop prototypes** – several rounds of development will take place, and this begins with a prototype (to assess viability, is it reasonable, etc.).
- **Design, develop, test** – work from an accepted prototype following create/deliver/support concepts (value stream).

Figure 28 is the technology adoption lifecycle (Moore, 2014). It suggests that the way an organisation uses innovation is reflected by its market position. Organisations that focus on innovation can be more disruptive, but face a higher risk of rejection, with products and services falling into the 'chasm'. Organisations that resist using new technology until they absolutely have to may miss opportunities and become obsolete.[36]

[36] *ITIL® 4: Digital and IT Strategy*, Figure 10.1. ITIL® is a registered trade mark of the PeopleCert group. Used under licence from PeopleCert. All rights reserved.

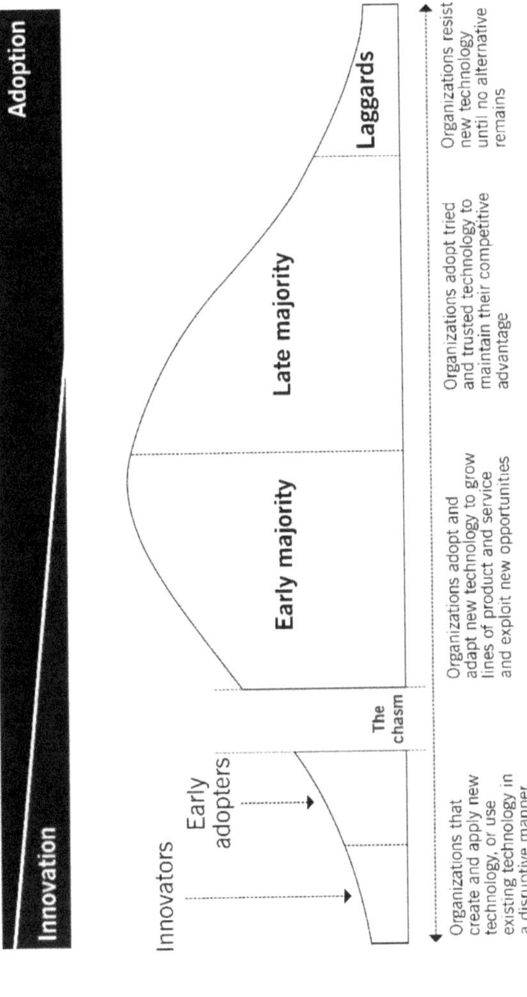

Figure 28: Technology adoption lifecycle

When an organisation learns about a new technology solution, it is often already in the early majority part of the technology adoption lifecycle. Vendors may sell the solution as the answer to all problems; organisations need to be wary and assess if the new solution actually meets their needs. It can help to ask:

- *"Will it become a mainstream solution?*
- *Will we be left behind if we do not adopt it?*
- *Is it significant enough to focus on instead of something else?"*

Figure 29 (Karu, 2019) shows the different stages of technology adoption. The silver bullet stage (*"it's the answer to all your problems")* relates to the early majority in Moore's lifecycle. Organisations need to be wary of investing in the shared utilization stage as there will be little advantage gained, and investing in legacy environments can do more harm than good. Investing in the novelty stage can provide the balance of risk and reward that many digital organisations seek.

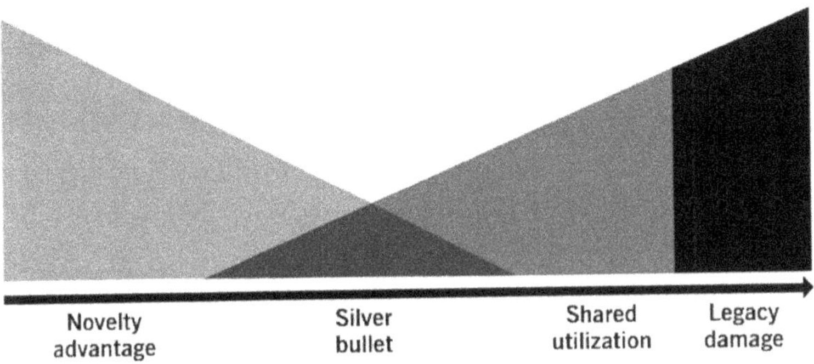

Figure 29: Stages of technology adoption[37]

Organisations need to actively research new and emerging technologies to help them understand where they might gain an advantage. This includes the following:

- Tracking trends in their ecosystem; what worked, what didn't?
- Understanding what is needed to make a solution successful.
- Being able to quantify the impact of emerging technologies on the organisation and its stakeholders, and how much it will cost.
- Understanding their business and operating models so that the impact of a new solution is understood.
- Being able to test a new technology or solution.

---

[37] *ITIL® 4: Digital and IT Strategy*, Figure 10.2. ITIL® is a registered trade mark of the PeopleCert group. Used under licence from PeopleCert. All rights reserved.

The last thing an organisation should have is a surprise. If you find out about a new solution after your competitors, you're already behind the curve in terms of potential adoption. This can lead to rushed decisions and poor payback.

Building an innovation-supporting culture

As with any cultural change, this is a long-term process, not a short project. It requires support from all levels and leadership to demonstrate correct behaviours. The table below outlines some of the key recommendations to create an innovation-supporting culture.

Table 27: Innovation-supporting culture

Recommendation	Consider…
Educate executives	Change leaders can help executives understand skills gaps, and what needs to change to get effective buy-in.
Harness workforce and talent management	This can include helping the practice recruit the right people, onboard them into the innovation culture, and provide training and support for existing employees.
Evangelise digital technology opportunities	Digital leaders in the organisation need to make sure everyone is aware of the possibilities of emerging technologies, and that employees have the skills to use them.

Provide learning tools	This can include internal and external training, knowledge bases and FAQs; whatever is needed to share knowledge within the organisation.
Give employees time to learn	As well as providing tools, employees need time to learn and reflect. How might they apply what they have learned to their role and day-to-day activities?
Provide freedom to experiment	Create a culture where it is safe to fail, and lessons are learned (fail fast and often, but don't keep failing in the same way!).
Encourage teams to incorporate learning	Allow 'slack' in the system to give employees time to share and incorporate learning. From the DevOps world comes the saying that 'improving daily work is more important than doing daily work'.
Establish a market intelligence practice	This will allow everyone to understand their customers, market and competitors. It will help them put learning and new technologies into the context of their environment.

One of the businesses that I founded is focused on training. It sells elearning for service management professionals. One trend that we've seen with our corporate clients is team leaders or managers who purchase licences but don't give their staff any time to study, or track whether training has been completed. They are making some investment in education, but without providing time and space to learn they will not see a good return on investment. We've made some changes to our products and services such as putting reporting into the manager's portal, but ultimately we can't influence their culture. As a service provider, that's a frustrating position to be in.

Approaches to innovation

Having a process for managing innovation allows ideas to be handled in a repeatable, consistent way. This allows innovations to be measured individually, but also compared with each other to judge success over time. We're going to look at four approaches to innovation:

- Managed chaos and distributed experimentation.
- Crowdsourced learning.
- Purposeful innovation.
- Continual learning.

Managed chaos and distributed experimentation

Managed chaos (also referred to as 'bounded instability') suggests that organisations are most successful when they empower employees and leaders and use self-organising teams to adapt to a volatile world. Managed chaos (Tom Peters, 1988) focuses on the organisation as an ecosystem of interdependent systems and networks, rather than a series of tasks to be micro-managed. Rather than looking for the root cause of an organisational problem, we can instead look for big-picture patterns that encourage or prevent the behaviours we want.

Managed chaos is built on self-organising teams and requires a high level of trust. The organisation becomes organic, sometimes referred to as a fractal organisation. This is the opposite of traditional 'command and control', top-down management. To begin the transition to managed chaos, organisations will need to:

- Set a vision for innovation;
- Hire the right people (looking for skills like curiosity and independence);
- Allow employees to conduct experiments across the organisation, not just in an innovation silo;
- Understand how to measure success;
- Use data-driven decision making; and
- Establish legal and ethical principles to underpin experimentation.

Crowdsourced learning

Crowdsourcing is the activity of giving tasks to a large group of people or to the general public, for example by asking for help on the Internet.[38]

Perhaps counter-intuitively, crowdsourcing can generate more and better innovation ideas than well-funded internal research and development teams. Crowdsourcing attracts greater numbers and may include people who use (or want to use) a product or service. These participants will have strong ideas about how something should work. Crowdsourcing can include working with user communities, or creating competitions and contests that are shared online. The competition includes a challenge, any relevant parameters, a deadline and often a financial reward. However, some organisations still view crowdsourcing as risky and are suspicious of ideas from outside the organisation. To ensure crowdsourcing is effective, consider:

- Redefining the role of research and development – allow teams to support the crowdsourcing effort and help state the challenge;
- Defining the problem as specifically as possible;
- Designing attractive, appropriate rewards; and
- Understanding the legal and intellectual property implications.

Purposeful innovation

Purposeful innovation is the *"systematic practice of innovation that results from focus, direction, and intentional*

---

[38]Source: *https://dictionary.cambridge.org/dictionary/english/crowdsourcing*.

opportunity mining". It suggests that innovation can be managed like any other business activity. Drucker (2002) suggests seven areas where innovation efforts should be focused:

- Unexpected occurrences.
- Incongruities.
- Process needs.
- Industry and market changes.
- Demographic changes.
- Changes in perception.
- New knowledge.

Continual learning

If we accept that technology and our environment are changing quickly, we must accept the need for continual learning. As disruption and innovation take place, the knowledge that helped us yesterday will not help us today. To adopt continual learning, it must be embraced at all levels of the organisation:

- Leaders need to identify the skills that support the organisation's vision and strategic goals.
- Teams need time and structure to share experience and incorporate lessons learned.
- Individuals need time and resources to learn new things.

CHAPTER 7: CREATING A DIGITAL STRATEGY

In this chapter, we'll learn more about the steps and techniques used to define and advocate for a digital and IT strategy. This chapter includes:

- Using a digital readiness assessment and performing a gap analysis;
- Defining and communicating a vision and a strategy; and
- Using a business case to advocate for a digital and IT strategy.

Digital readiness assessments

I have a problem with the term 'digital transformation'. First, because it implies that digital is itself a goal, rather than focusing on the outcomes that digital technologies can support. And second, because transformation implies a single, world-changing event – the caterpillar becomes the butterfly and flies away. Many of the digital transformation projects I've been around have had a set timeline, lots of investment in external consultants, and not much in the way of results. The organisation runs out of time or money, or focus just moves to the next big thing.

> The chapters in this book and my own experience suggest a different approach will yield better results. Focusing on culture, iteration and building an organisation that is continually changing and adapting will lead to success. We're stuck with 'digital transformation' as the term is commonly adopted, but think carefully about what it means if you are involved in any transformation programme.

Gartner data suggests that only 25% of organisations will successfully target new ways of working in 80% of their initiatives. Using a digital readiness assessment can help an organisation maximise its chances of success in digitalisation initiatives. Effective assessments highlight gaps and show where an organisation needs to prioritise its efforts. A digital readiness assessment can:

- Analyse the internal and external environment and how they might change;
- Assess the organisation's current position, capabilities and resources;
- Provide a baseline for how to move towards organisational goals; and
- Support the organisation as it prioritises strategic objectives and moves towards its future state.

The key activities in a readiness assessment are to evaluate the current capabilities, carry out a gap analysis and then produce an output including risks and challenges.

Table 28 explains these activities in more detail.

Table 28: Digital readiness assessments

Evaluate current capabilities	This can be carried out by internal or external assessors, and will include the following: • Strategy and digital positioning – is there a digital transformation vision? Is it shared? • Value streams, practices and processes – what is their maturity and impact on the digital business? • Information and technology – is automation in place? Is digital technology used to benefit the customer and the organisation? • Organisational development and learning – what are the hiring and onboarding practices? Are there opportunities for growth? • Risk management – are business/digital risks and opportunities understood? Are they balanced? • Innovation – is it valued, managed and integrated across the organisation?
Gap analysis	A gap analysis assesses organisational strengths and weaknesses and defines actionable improvements for the short, medium and long term. It should include: • Objectives/desired future state;

	• Current state for each objective; and • Actions and resources needed to close the gap between current and future state.
Output	The output will usually contain sections such as: • Cultural readiness; • Skills assessment results; • Current level of innovation/innovation appetite; • Current level of automation; • Current level of value stream mapping and automation; • Current products and services and their suitability for digitisation; • Customer personas/profiles; • Leadership style; and • Current controls and governance.

There are some risks and challenges associated with digital readiness assessments. An assessment can be too complex or too simplistic; both of these scenarios may deliver unhelpful results. They may be too technology focused, and miss crucial elements such as culture, practices, leadership, etc. Some assessments take too general an approach to risk assessment and don't include the risks that are unique to digital initiatives. As with any assessment, the time spent in planning and preparation will be rewarded with more accurate results.

Defining and communicating a vision and strategy

Many organisations now articulate a vision and a purpose for what they do. A purpose describes the reason an organisation exists (in other words, its core business). A vision is more aspirational, looking at what an organisation would like to be in the future and the objectives it aims to achieve (think about Banksbest wanting to be a 'digital first' provider).

An organisation's business strategy will address both the vision and the purpose. It should outline how they will be delivered and through which initiatives, providing information that will feed down into functional strategies for areas such as marketing, finance, etc.

The digital and IT strategy must be aligned with the business strategy and the organisation's overall vision and purpose. The digital strategy will define a future state and how this will contribute to supporting customer needs. A digital vision can help promote transformation and understanding.

Confirming the scope of the vision

A team can only define a vision for areas within its own scope. If a team or group tries to define a strategy for an area it doesn't have any control over, the strategy is highly likely to fail due to their lack of influence. The strategy management practice will ensure that any vision or strategy is properly scoped and led with the appropriate level of authority.

The only exceptions to this would be applied by an organisation's governance, for example to:

- Include an area in a strategy that wouldn't normally be in scope; or

- To fund or make resources available for something that would normally be out of scope which will allow it to be included.

Defining the vision

If the vision has been defined before any type of assessment has been carried out, it will need to be reviewed and possibly updated after an assessment.

It's helpful to define a vision as a group to make sure it reflects more than just one person's opinion; include all stakeholders with authority over any aspect of the strategy. This can be challenging when different individuals and teams have different perspectives, so it may help to have an independent facilitator there to keep things on track.

The purpose of the vision is to define the desired future state of the organisation, which will be an input into strategy planning and implementation. Some organisations will have an internal and external version of their vision statement: one that is suitable for marketing purposes and can be shared with customers, and one that may have a more internal focus (such as profitability goals or an exit plan).

For a vision definition workshop, consider these points:

- Include a representative from each business area (ideally, a senior member).
- Have limited numbers (8–12 people).
- Break into small groups, then have a representative for each group.
- Be aware of political dynamics and sensitivities.
- Ensure all voices are heard and each person has an equal voice.

- Set the threshold for decisions – unanimous decisions, or as allowed by organisation culture (consensus).
- All concerns should be addressed.
- Include external stakeholders only if they are responsible for some aspect of the strategy.

Further guidelines for crafting a vision are as follows:

- Separate it from the purpose (unless the vision is to change the purpose!).
- Be concise, unambiguous and direct – test the vision on different people to be sure it's clear.
- Be aspirational and inspiring to help build motivation.
- Align with the organisation's core beliefs, and be consistent with core behaviours and values.
- Be unique and specific.
- Focus on the organisation, customer experiences, new business models, etc., not just technology; base the vision on a deep understanding of the organisation's current or planned consumers.
- Show intent and the desired outcome, allowing freedom and flexibility for the teams who will work towards the vision.
- Set a date (make it time-bound) to create urgency.

Strategy planning

Creating a strategy isn't a one-off activity. Strategic activities are ongoing and need to adapt to changes in both internal and external factors. An organisation that only reviews its strategy once a year may find that it is in a very reactive position and has missed opportunities.

Strategy planning doesn't have to be complex and time consuming. When we study strategy planning, it can seem daunting – so many activities to complete.

I work in small organisations. Our strategy planning leads to the same outputs and outcomes, but the process is adjusted to suit the size of the organisation. For example, in my training business we get pretty much the whole team together and we use a spider diagram to go round each area of the business. We cover legal, finance, customer support, marketing, sales, course production, and technology to see what needs to change to meet our business goals. We create lists of actions and everyone knows where we're going.

I should also add that our strategy often lasts about three months before something in our market changes. We've learned to be adaptable!

Strategic planning is an iterative process. Each organisation will need to find a balance between the time and effort it puts into creating and reviewing its strategy and the potential opportunity costs associated with a delay. Different levels of the organisation may review their strategies at different times; the overall business strategy may be reviewed and updated less frequently than functional unit strategies.

Figure 30 shows the variability of planning and review cycles. An organisation has not changed its purpose and vision for five years. In year one, two strategic initiatives are launched, but these are superseded by two new initiatives in year two, perhaps because of an environmental change. After this, more frequent reviews are carried out and initiatives become more fragmented. Then, as the environment stabilises, the strategy cycle lengthens again.[39]

[39] *ITIL® 4: Digital and IT Strategy*, Figure 5.1. ITIL® is a registered trade mark of the PeopleCert group. Used under licence from PeopleCert. All rights reserved.

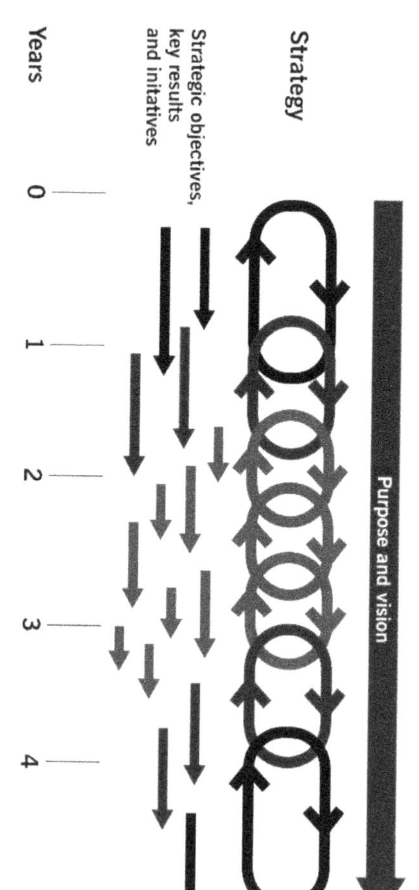

Figure 30: Strategy cycles

A strategy can be thought of as a system of artefacts. It needs to have a structure that supports the overall business model, architecture, structure and governance. Typical artefacts associated with a strategy include:

- *"Strategic assessment*
- *Positioning statement or analysis*
- *Several scenarios indicating likely outcomes if certain variables are changed*
- *Vision*
- *Business model*
- *Financial analyses of all options*
- *Plan, or several related plans*
- *Project and product portfolio, often together with an application portfolio*
- *Detailed architecture of the future-state organization, infrastructure, solution, or some other aspect of the strategy*
- *Risk analysis and treatment options"*

These artefacts should be managed individually rather than as a single document. This makes them easier to use and update and can help protect sensitive information. A collaboration tool or document management system should be used (where present).

Different stakeholders will have access to different strategy artefacts depending on their role. The artefacts can be used as a dynamic management tool, with elements included in a variety of dashboards, progress reports, etc. This approach means a strategy is easier to consume rather than a huge document that no one will read. Elements of a strategy document may include:

- Purpose and vision
- Scope and authority
- Context
- Objectives and key results
- Budget and investment
- Principles
- Capabilities
- Roadmap
- Initiative details

Large organisations may have a decentralised strategy planning approach with multiple strategies managed by different groups or executives. Some organisations have a centralised approach managed by a strategy team or department. Whatever approach is followed, the strategy must not be developed in isolation.

Strategy oversight and controls

The governing body has oversight of the organisational strategy. Executives define the strategy for their area of responsibility, linking back to the overall strategy, vision and purpose. Strategic controls should include:

- *"Measuring and reporting the progress of strategic initiatives*
- *Measuring and reporting whether the strategy is achieving its objectives*
- *Evaluating whether the strategy is still relevant in its changing environment*

- *Detecting unintended consequences*
- *Regular stakeholder meetings to consider the above, and determine whether action is required to change the strategy or any part of a related strategic initiative*
- *Reporting to other strategy owners whose strategy is linked to this one*
- *Checks against the enterprise strategy, to ensure that stakeholders do not make the organization deviate from its desired position or objectives"*

Using a business case for Digital and IT Strategy

A strategy can be viewed as a high-level type of business case. It articulates the organisational vision, shows what would happen if nothing changed in the organisation, and defines options for action with costs, risks and expected outcomes.

The proposed initiatives in the strategy will be supported by individual, more detailed business cases to allow them to be assessed, prioritised and, if approved, funded. Each individual business case must link back to the overall strategy, vision and purpose for the organisation. Business cases should reflect the strategy's structure to allow options to be compared.

Quantifying the value of a digital or IT strategy

The value of a strategy is how well it supports the organisation's purpose and vision, and enables the achievement of desired outcome(s). The business case will outline the initiatives that the organisation could pursue, as well as those that it will not pursue, and the opportunity costs associated with these. The non-financial value for the organisation should also be addressed, for example will it lead to a change in how it is perceived by consumers? These areas should be documented:

- **Costs** – capital investments, operational expenses, resource use, technology costs, compliance costs, innovation/R&D costs, partnership/supplier costs.
- **Risks** – detail negative risks, their impact and treatment for assessment by stakeholder.
- **Returns and benefits** – as a result of a strategy investment (calculated by the cost subtracted from the benefit). It can be difficult to define non-financial costs and benefits.
- **Opportunity costs** – the impact on the organisation if the business case is rejected or another option is chosen, including both financial and non-financial impact.

Communicating the business case

Communicating the strategy to stakeholders who are expected to implement it is different from communicating the business case to those who are expected to fund it. The right person must get the right message.

Intended audience

Business cases allow key decision makers to approve, reject or modify a course of action. Their role is not to raise general awareness of the overall strategy. The audience of the business case will typically include:

- Stakeholders who are expected to approve or fund the initiative; and

- Advisors to those stakeholders, including subject matter experts where needed.

The audience for the business case is defined by the scope of the initiative or the strategy. If the business case is presented to the wrong audience, an incorrect decision may be made.

Timing

The business case will reflect the timing of the initiative and be linked to the overall strategy review cycles. If a strategy includes multiple initiatives, each one will need its own business case, including the initiative start and end date and key checkpoints in between. When the strategy is reviewed, the business cases associated with it will also need to be reviewed.

If a business case is rejected or found to be no longer viable when it is reviewed, the strategy may also need to be reviewed and revised. After an initiative has been completed, it needs to be measured and reviewed against the original business case to confirm whether it was a success. This can lead to improvements to the initiative itself, and to the organisation's business case and planning processes.

Format

Most organisations have a template for business cases; if you don't have access to a template, you'll find many examples online. They will typically include the following sections:

- **Executive summary:** concise summary of the business case.
- **Introduction.**

- **Problem statement:** clear, objective description of the problem being solved.
- **Analysis:** providing more detail about the problem to help the business case reader to understand more about the context.
- **Discussion of possible options:** identify potential solutions to the problem described.
- **Benefits:** why it would be a good idea to approve the recommended action in the business case.
- **Cost:** including resource requirements.
- **Likely timescale.**
- **Anticipated return on investment, with supporting information and assumptions.**
- **Risk:** possible negative outcomes, and factors that might prevent successful implementation.
- **Recommendations:** for the project and how it is to be conducted.
- **Details of the chosen option.**
- **Conclusion:** summary and reminder of why it is essential to address the problem.

At Banksbest, Lucy Jones has been asked to review the business case for the adoption of biometric identification such as voice recognition and fingerprints. Recreate these business case sections for her:

- **Problem statement:** what is the problem being solved?
- **Risk:** what are the possible negative outcomes?

You can make assumptions where you need additional information.

Obtain and manage feedback

Each business case will reflect the strategy it aims to support. Stakeholders reviewing a business case may not have been involved with the strategy definition and can use the business case approval process to try to influence the strategy itself.

It is important to try to involve all stakeholders in the strategy definition so that business cases can be reviewed objectively.

Using business cases ensures that there is recorded, auditable approval for actions taken and funding allocated to strategic initiatives. The business case provides clarity around funding and what resources are available, and helps confirm the overall strategic direction by validating the actions taken to support it.

Any feedback about a business case or the overall strategic direction can be used in the strategy review process.

Dealing with resistance

The best way to overcome resistance is to involve stakeholders in the process, allowing them to feel ownership and reducing the impression that something is being forced onto them. However, many organisations develop their strategy with a small number of senior stakeholders, leading to resistance from managers who haven't been involved.

A better approach is to develop strategies collaboratively so that the digital and IT strategy, for example, can clearly reflect its links to the overall business strategy and any dependencies that exist. Influence, cooperation and education between different areas of the organisation are essential, along with a strong mandate and consistent approach from the organisation's executive.

The ITIL® 4 organizational change management practice recommends:

- Education and awareness programmes;
- Reassuring employees of their continued employment;
- Creation of safe working environments;
- Negotiation;
- Creating incentives to support the programme; and
- Reskilling programmes.

CHAPTER 8: IMPLEMENTING A DIGITAL AND IT STRATEGY

In this chapter, we'll look at how to take your strategy from 'on the page' to being fully implemented in the organisation. This includes:

- Defining operating models for digital organisations;
- The architecture management practice;
- The workforce and talent management practice;
- Leadership skills in a digital organisation;
- Approaches for strategy coordination and implementation;
- The parallel operating model;
- Assessing a successful digital and IT strategy; and
- Digital transformation activities.

Operating models

An operating model is defined within the ITIL publications as a *"conceptual and/or visual representation of how an organization co-creates value with its customers and other stakeholders, as well as how the organization runs itself"*. Business models (we studied these earlier) show how an organisation will capture business value. Operating models show how an organisation will structure and run itself to create value.

An operating model represents a series of practices and choices; it defines how the organisation will deliver its value proposition and maintain its market position. An operating model is a tool that is used to support the design and configuration of how the organisation will work. It has two key themes:

- The key work that takes place to support the organisation's value streams.
- The context in which work is performed, which includes:
    - Partners and suppliers;
    - Where work is located;
    - What assets are used to perform work;
    - Organisation structure, skills, decision making, etc.;
    - Supporting technology; and
    - Performance measures and metrics.

Figure 31 shows the operating model canvas, organised around value delivery.

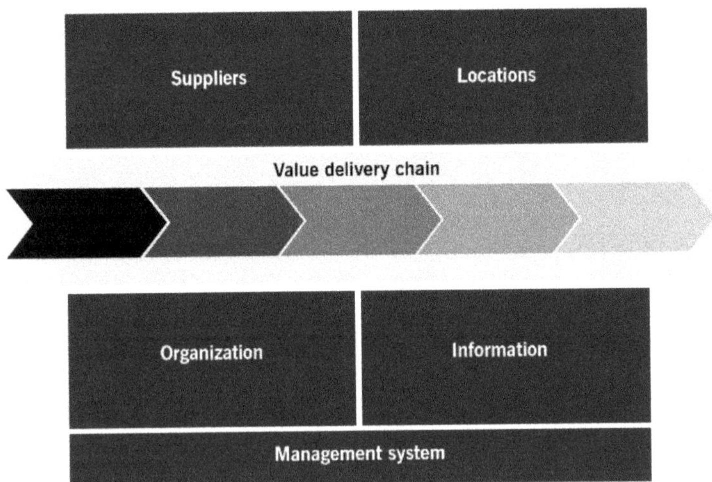

Figure 31: Operating model canvas[40]

An operating model for a digital organisation is very similar to a 'normal' organisational operating model. It will include:

- How value is created;
- Value streams;
- People, process and technology that support value streams;
- Partners and contracts;
- Culture;
- Consumers, products and services;
- Project, service and product portfolios; and

40 *ITIL® 4: Digital and IT Strategy*, Figure 2.9. From Campbell, A., Gutierrez, M. and Lancelott, M. (2017) Operating Model Canvas. Van Haren Publishing. ITIL® is a registered trade mark of the PeopleCert group.

- Investment in value streams and portfolios.

The differences or information that may be added for a digital organisation include emerging technologies, more emphasis on innovation and experimentation, and more agile processes and culture. ITIL® 4 uses the service value chain to represent an operating model.

A digital business needs to be flexible and responsive to rapidly respond to market conditions and to adopt new, emerging practices and technology to provide sustained competitive advantage. Traditional hierarchical structures are being replaced by flatter structures, and reduced time to market, agile ways of working, etc. are more widely adopted. The shift to a product model is different to traditional project management, and customer expectations are higher.

To succeed, an organisation must focus on:

- Maintaining strategic alignment and accountability across teams, departments and divisions;
- A common and communicated understanding of value, outcomes, costs and risks (VOCR);
- A collaborative approach; and
- A culture and an executive who support learning.

Practice: Architecture management

Purpose

The purpose of the architecture management practice is to *"explain the different elements that form an organization"*. It focuses on how elements interrelate to support current and future organisational objectives. The practice will be supported by principles, standards and tools for architecture management.

There are different layers of organisational architecture:

- Business
- Product and service
- Information systems
- Technology
- Environmental

The organisational strategy and vision will define how the organisation manages the architectural layers. The scope of the practice will be dictated by the nature of the organisation and also sourcing choices (such as outsourcing for technical elements). If technology is outsourced, the external supplier may manage the lower levels of the technology architecture. The procuring organisation would focus on supplier performance and quality assurance.

Figure 32 shows how the architecture levels need to be mapped across the four dimensions of service management.

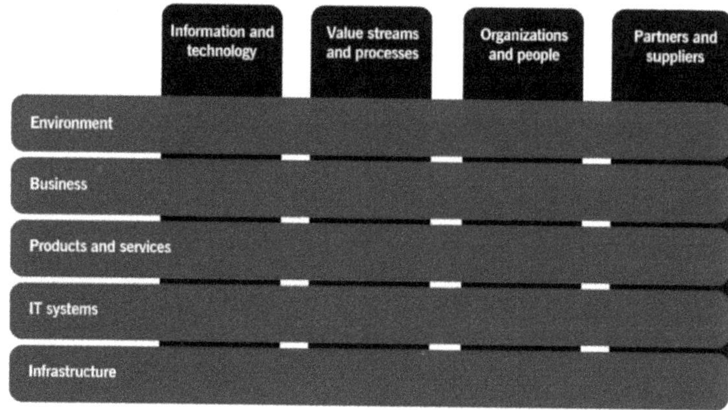

Figure 32: Architecture layers and the four dimensions of service management[41]

The architecture that is adopted must support the organisation's strategic goals, and be continually optimised to meet changing requirements. To achieve this, the current architecture is analysed to create a baseline. Any gaps are identified and if necessary, a new target model is created to show how gaps can be addressed. The organisation can then look at moving from its current architecture to a future state that will fully meet its needs; all supported of course by a business case.

Practice success factors

There are two PSFs defined for the architecture management practice:

---

[41] *ITIL® 4 Architecture Management Practice Guide*, Figure 2.1. ITIL® is a registered trade mark of the PeopleCert group. Used under licence from PeopleCert. All rights reserved.

- Ensure that the organization's strategy is supported with a target architecture.
- Ensure that the organization's architecture is continually evolving to the target state.

Table 29: Architecture management practice success factors

PSF: Ensure that the organization's strategy is supported with a target architecture
The target reference model for the organisation's architecture will ensure it supports the overall strategy and provides assurance that the strategy can be achieved. The target reference model will be developed after reviewing: • The current organisational strategy and performance; • Current architecture and any benefits or constraints; • Major pain points related to architecture; • Portfolios and plans; • Environmental factors and trends; and • Technology factors and trends, risks and opportunities. This information can be used to develop an architecture that will support the organisation's current and future goals.
PSF: Ensure the organization's architecture is continually evolving to the target state
As with most organisational assets, the architecture will not stay the same and needs to evolve as business goals

change. An architectural roadmap is a useful tool to help define how the architecture will remain aligned with changing requirements. A roadmap will include *"recommendations and requirements for the taxonomy, standards, guidelines, procedures, templates, and tools that would use for any architecturally important initiative"*.

Changes to the architecture will be managed using project or programme management, and using the organisation's architectural standards. Any change to the service value system that deploys new or changed components, services or architecture changes will need to be linked to architecture management so that the impact can be understood.

The overall target architecture may never be achieved (or may change before it is fully achieved), but it is important to have a goal to aim towards.

There is an opportunity cost associated with poor architecture management in any organisation. Having limited understanding of the architecture that supports current products and services limits how innovative an organisation can be in proposing new ideas. Many organisations that I've worked with are frightened to make too many changes, as they're not able to fully understand the consequences for live products and services that are currently working well. This lack of understanding can also be a risk associated with outsourcing all or part of the IT estate. If the outsourcing organisation isn't careful, it will lose the knowledge and skills it needs and become locked in to its supplier.

Practice: Workforce and talent management

Purpose

The purpose of the workforce and talent management practice is to *"ensure that the organization has the right people, with the appropriate skills and knowledge, in the correct roles to support its business objectives"*.

This practice is focused on the effective management of the organization and people dimension of ITIL® 4. People and knowledge are highly valuable assets for any organisation.

Workforce and talent management activities include:

- Planning
- Recruitment
- Onboarding
- Learning and development
- Performance measurement
- Succession planning

If you're looking for an improvement opportunity in your own organisation, I highly recommend taking a look at the onboarding and offboarding procedures. I'm stunned that these are still such a hot topic, but after more than 20 years in ITSM I still see problems here. For example, a friend of mine joined an organisation but waited two weeks (fully paid) to get security clearance to begin his role. No other use was made of his time. Another friend left a remote position and is still in possession of the laptop and mobile phone he was issued.

The post-pandemic shift to remote working makes this all the more critical. How we onboard people sets the tone for their employment; we don't get a second chance to make a first impression. It's very nice to have a branded company water bottle and some chocolate, but do you have what you need to do the job?

Workforce and talent management will usually be supported by specialised roles and organisational structures. In larger organisations there will often be a dedicated team, although this can be organised in different ways. Some organisations separate IT recruitment and talent management from their workforce and talent management team, allowing IT managers to fulfil this role and recruit the specialist skills that they need. If this is the case, IT managers still need to receive support and guidance to make sure they follow any necessary policies or regulations.

> You've been asked by Banksbest to create an employee onboarding and offboarding process for staff working in the customer services technical specialist team. Create a checklist for each process – what activities need to happen?
>
> How would you measure the effectiveness of these processes?

VUCA environments need a workforce and talent management practice that can adapt to changing requirements. The practice needs to recognise that:

- *"Organizations are open systems, their relationships with other systems cannot be ignored*
- *Organizational strategies continually evolve, and so should the associated HR strategy*
- *Digital technologies change the way organizations work and the skills that organizations need*
- *Decisions should be driven by principles, not rules*
- *Organizations should recognize and embrace complexity and complexity-driven heuristics*
- *Organizational agility, adaptability, and efficiency should be enabled by the organizational structure and management practices*
- *Workforce and talent management is the responsibility of every team, manager, and leader in the organization, not only HR professionals"*

Practice success factors

There are three PSFs defined for the workforce and talent management practice:

- *"Ensuring continual alignment of the workforce and talent management approach to the organization's business strategy*
- *Ensuring that motivated and competent people effectively contribute to the achievement of organizational objectives*
- *Ensuring the administrative processes for this practice effectively support the organizational strategy and objectives"*

Table 30: Workforce and talent management practice success factors

PSF: Ensuring continual alignment of the workforce and talent management approach to the organization's business strategy
Workforce and talent management needs to adopt an agile approach so that goals can be refined and adjusted when necessary. This includes: • Agile and efficient organisational structures (such as multidisciplinary teams); • An agile, creative, efficient culture; • Effective leadership approaches such as servant leadership; and • Ongoing planning for changes in the workforce.

Morgan (2015) proposed 14 principles for future organisations that are particularly relevant for workforce and talent management:

- Globally distributed, with smaller teams.
- Connected workforce.
- Intrapreneurial.
- Operates like a small company.
- Focuses on 'want' instead of 'need' (create a place where people want to work, not somewhere they come because they need a job).
- Adapt to change faster.
- Innovate everywhere.
- Operate in the Cloud.
- Have more women in senior management roles.
- Have a flatter structure.
- Tell stories.
- Democratise learning.
- Shift from profit to prosperity.
- Adapt to the future employee and manager.[42]

PSF: Ensuring that motivated and competent people effectively contribute to the achievement of organizational objectives

Workforce and talent management supports the achievement of organisational objectives through:

[42] Read more here: *https://medium.com/jacob-morgan/the-14-principles-of-the-future-organization-a8de78250711*.

- Employee journey management;
- Supporting continual learning and development;
- Maintaining a healthy organisational culture; and
- Conscious leadership.

Effective workforce and talent management will then lead to these outcomes:

- An understanding of the organisational workforce and competency needs.
- Availability of competencies when required.
- Shared organisational values and principles.
- A workplace that is safe, supports autonomy and professional and purposeful development, and provides purpose.
- Physical, social and work environments that are optimised for effective contribution to organisational objectives, culture and principles.

PSF: Ensuring the administrative processes for this practice effectively support the organizational strategy and objectives

Workforce and talent management helps an organisation understand what is available from its current workforce (numbers, competencies, performance, costs, etc.) and ensures compliance with legislation and regulations.

The practice administration creates a level of control, conformance and compliance, but should not add unnecessary bureaucracy. The ITIL guiding principles can help deliver an efficient approach:

- **Focus on value** – introduce controls that contribute to value creation.
- **Think and work holistically** – analyse/optimise controls right across the organisation.
- **Progress iteratively with feedback** – listen to feedback, and optimise procedures and controls.
- **Optimize and automate** – automate to minimise effort, costs, distractions.

Skills for digital leaders

In this section, we'll review:

- Digital mindset;
- Communication;
- Relationship management;
- Evaluating emerging technology;
- Agile management;
- Education and learning;
- Defining strategic metrics;
- Managing diverse environments;
- Operationalising strategy; and
- Business and technology management skills.

Digital mindset

ITIL defines a digital mindset as a *"set of attitudes and behaviors that cause someone to constantly consider the possibilities that digital technology offers their organization and its stakeholders and look for ways to make those possibilities real"*.

A digital (or 'growth') mindset isn't just displayed at work; you may be able to think of people in your family or social circle who display this kind of entrepreneurial approach, always looking at new possibilities and ways of doing things.

Someone with a digital mindset understands how technology changes (or could change) how people work and live. At work, they will see how technology can help the organisation achieve its strategic goals.

Successful digital organisations need leaders who can balance the use of technology with the 'human' element of business and recognise that changes affect people professionally, personally and socially. These types of organisation have some consistent characteristics:

- Leaders facilitate the creation of a vision or purpose and empower teams to act.
- Teams are encouraged to challenge the way things work and propose something better.
- Leaders understand that changes take time and the organisational culture is an integral part of making them successful. Leaders continually consider culture and the human impact of change.
- Leaders relinquish control of their teams' activities and focus on removing constraints and facilitating decisions.
- Measures of productivity include the achievement of outcomes, not just the quality of outputs.
- Safety is central, both physical and psychological.
- Leaders create a level of stability that allows change to take place.
- Leaders question ideas and base decisions on data.

- Digital leaders allow teams to self-organise and self-manage; they focus on outcomes and results for stakeholders.

Digital leaders challenge their own assumptions about how they and others work. A mindset is based on values and beliefs. It isn't always easy to hire or develop a mindset, so some organisations will focus on developing staff into leadership roles if they show the right values.

Some organisations will find they don't have people with the right mindset to begin a transformation initiative. The leaders in these organisations will need to:

- Change their definition of 'leadership' and look at how they hire for leadership positions;
- Get executive support for cultural changes and new ways of working;
- Hire people with experience of change;
- Be ready to hear things that make them uncomfortable; and
- Create and maintain measures, behaviours and language that support the new vision and desired cultural change.

Communication

We've already said in several chapters of this book that a strategy can't be developed in isolation. It needs to be shared with stakeholders and explained clearly if it is to be successfully adopted in the organisation. Excellent communication is a fundamental requirement for leaders. They must be able to:

- Communicate at every level of the organisation;

- Plan and deploy a communication strategy;
- Analyse feedback to ensure effective communication;
- Practise transparency with stakeholders – update frequently; and
- Emphasise outcomes (not performance).

Relationship management

Organisational change relies on collaboration and coordination to be successful. Digital leaders rely on alignment, communication and collaboration between stakeholders right across the organisation. Relationship management is more than just a skill; it is an organisational capability that leaders need to support and nurture. Effective relationship management via the relationship management practice will help:

- Establish shared or mutually recognised goals;
- Facilitate a culture of no-blame cooperation and collaboration;
- Promote continual learning among and between teams;
- Set guidelines and policies for open and transparent communication; and
- Define how to identify, prevent and mediate in conflict situations.

For digital leaders in particular, relationship management will help them link strategic objectives with other objectives across the organisation, providing a holistic set of goals.

Evaluate emerging technology

Digital leaders need to understand technology and industry trends and, more importantly, evaluate them in the context of their own organisation. Are they a threat? An opportunity? Relevant? Not relevant right now?

To be able to do this effectively, leaders will need to understand the current business model, architecture, products, services, value proposition, operating model and value streams. In other words, all the elements that we've studied in this book help provide context for leaders as they evaluate technology and make decisions.

Agile management

Agile approaches to management can help reduce time to market and allow an organisation to respond to changes quickly and effectively. Agile management approaches include merging build and run cycles, reducing design and production timescales, and automating or outsourcing where appropriate. The cross-functional teams that are typically found in this type of organisation require different leaders than a more traditional, hierarchical organisation.

I'm seeing a lot of organisation embrace agile ways of working in software development. What they often find is that they experience friction once they need something from outside the IT department. For example, does the organisation have an agile financial management process that can support Agile development? Or is the organisation still focused on annual budget cycles and detailed business cases for investment? To get the full benefits from any new way of working, it needs to be assessed holistically and may require changes across the organisation.

Once the new ways of working spread outside the original team, the benefits are lost if other areas of the organisation don't change as well.

Education and learning

Education should be seen as an ongoing activity at the heart of success for digital organisations. Education helps leaders:

- Understand the changes occurring in their internal and external environments;
- Identify technology and industry trends, and how to exploit them;
- Learn about the mistakes of other organisations, and don't repeat them;
- Communicate details about the organisation's digital and IT strategy, and set expectations about the changes it will introduce;
- Inform stakeholders about how the use of new technologies will impact the organisation;
- Achieve higher levels of enthusiasm and buy-in for Digital and IT Strategy initiatives;
- Share basic concepts about how to build, manage, support and use new technologies; and
- Promote a sense of humility: no one in the organisation knows everything and knowledge should be shared.

A quick online search will show you that many organisations now offer courses in digital leadership. However, many of these offerings focus on technology, which can change and become out of date very quickly. Digital leaders need to focus on the skills and values that will help them fulfil their role (such as curiosity, data-based decision making, etc.) and then use ongoing research to keep on top of technology and technical trends.

As well as learning, leaders also need to teach and help educate other staff and stakeholders in the organisation. Education and training are vital; they will help organisations:

- Understand the reasons for changes;
- Link changes to strategic outcomes;
- Ensure that all stakeholders understand what is expected of them;
- Learn the new skills required to work within the new environment;
- Indicate how performance measurement will change;
- Indicate how success will be rewarded in the new environment; and
- Equip teams to assess their contribution to the new initiative.

Many of us hear the word 'training' and imagine a classroom and a tutor. In a digital organisation, training can take many forms, from informal communities of practice to elearning. Education in different forms will be offered to peers, managers, staff, shareholders, suppliers and consumers.

Doug Range is responsible for training customer service centre staff at Banksbest. He's brought you in to create a training plan to support the My Way project. You're going to do a training needs analysis and make some recommendations. Create a plan for:

- Assessing current skills;
- Identifying gaps; and
- What new skills are needed to support My Way, and how training should be delivered.

The table below shows guidance for an education programme sponsored by digital leaders.

Table 31: Education and training program for stakeholders[43]

Scope	*Audience*	*Purpose*
Strategic context	*Everyone*	*To explain the changes in the environment and what opportunities they represent for the organization. (Why are we doing this?)*

[43] *ITIL® 4: Digital and IT Strategy*, Table 6.1. ITIL® is a registered trade mark of the PeopleCert group. Used under licence from PeopleCert.

High-level overview of each strategic initiative and its outcomes	*Everyone*	*To highlight the overall vision for digital strategy in the organization and show why this work is so important. (Where are we going?)*
Detailed overview of each strategic initiative and its outcomes	*Senior and middle management, senior technical experts*	*To indicate the level of effort, what is required of each part of the organization, and how they will be measured. (What are we going to be doing?)*
Detailed description of the objectives and activities of each initiative	*Managers and staff involved in each initiative*	*To educate staff involved in the initiative about exactly what is expected of them, how they will be working, who they will be working with, what the outputs are and when they are expected, how everyday work will continue alongside this initiative, etc. (What am I going to be doing?)*
How to use the tools that form	*Practitioners (staff, partners, suppliers,*	*To educate and train those building the solution in how to use the tools available to them, and the*

part of each initiative	*contractors, etc.)*	*features and functionality of the technology being configured and implemented. (How will I be doing it?)*
How to work in the changed organization	*Managers and practitioners*	*To educate and train those using the new tools, processes, and working methods in how to do so effectively. (How has my job changed as a result of these changes?)*

Defining strategic metrics

Strategic metrics focus on outcomes, and the strategic objectives of the organisation. This can be a mindset shift for managers who are used to reporting on outputs and metrics including time, cost, etc. Strategic metrics should be developed that will act as indicators for:

- Tracking strategic initiatives (Are we on track?);
- Relevant and achievable strategy (Is change required?); and
- Achieving the anticipated benefits (Is change required?).

Managing diverse environments

Digital organisations are diverse in many ways: their staff, their ways of working and the technologies that they use. Leaders need to be able to coordinate and support collaboration across these diverse areas to support strategic objectives.

Operationalising strategy

Leaders in a strategic role may be in a unique and sometimes lonely and uncomfortable position. They need to be visionary, but also pragmatic. Digital leaders need to be able to combine imagination and application of new ideas. Digital leaders need to be encouraged and rewarded to thrive in this space.

We often think of leaders as being almost alien-like – visionaries from another planet whose behaviour and way of thinking is not the same as ours. Vision is wonderful, but effective leadership also needs to create an environment where execution is possible. As we said earlier in this book, innovation is only 'real' when it delivers value. Millions of good ideas never make it off the page, and the organisation that 'wins' is the organisation that gets things done. A good friend of mine who is a very successful entrepreneur says that running a business requires vision, but also relentless focus on the detail. A challenging mix, and not one that everyone can achieve.

Business and technology management skills

After finishing this section, you may be wondering who these giants are who work as digital leaders. Can we ever hope to fill these shoes? Traditional IT roles are often very specialised, but digital leaders need to be business leaders as well and fully understand their organisation. Digital leaders need to be comfortable with:

- Finance
- Marketing
- Business operations
- Information security
- Ways of working
- Technology management

Even the most accomplished leader will need to adopt a lifelong learning approach to stay relevant in their role.

Strategy coordination and implementation approaches

Creating a strategy is almost the easy part. Implementing it can be much more of a challenge. History tends to be written by the winners, so the information available to the industry tends to be more focused on success stories than what went wrong.

Strategic plans are, ultimately, implemented by teams. An organisation's leaders will provide funding, ensure resources are available and remove any obstacles. Team managers need to decide how best to implement plans and manage implementation actions.

Table 32 shows some of the key characteristics of organisations that are successful in achieving their strategic goals.

Table 32: Key organisational characteristics for a successful strategy implementation

Clear and consistent communication of the vision	The context and the vision are communicated frequently in multiple formats. The message is pervasive at all organisational levels and is supported by examples and stories.
Decision-making is at the team level	Leadership provides direction/intent, which defines the operational boundaries of team decisions. Leaders then provide quick, decisive decisions on elements beyond the teams' authority.
Focus on fewer initiatives	Better work (efficient, effective, quality) can be done when there are less distractions and fewer projects in-flight. These organisations will have a strategically based, prioritised backlog.
Remove barriers to progress	This can include: • Providing collaboration tools; • Approving resources; • Clearly communicating what's important;

	• Removing unnecessary steps or approvals; • Streamlining reporting; and • Providing mentorship and coaching. Digital leaders, team leaders and managers should continually review their environments for any new barriers.
Allow large transformations to be carried out incrementally or all at once	Teams may need to be restructured to improve workflow, communication and collaboration.
Deal with setbacks	Any transformation will include some setbacks. Leaders need to overcome doubt and accept that sometimes things get worse before they improve. Patience is important, as is retaining focus on the vision.
Effective executive leadership	Leaders will help guide teams through the organisational change, and will reinforce the vision during all stages of the transformation.

Approaches to change

The Satir model shown in Figure 33 is used to describe the stages that an individual, a team or an organisation will go through in response to a significant change.

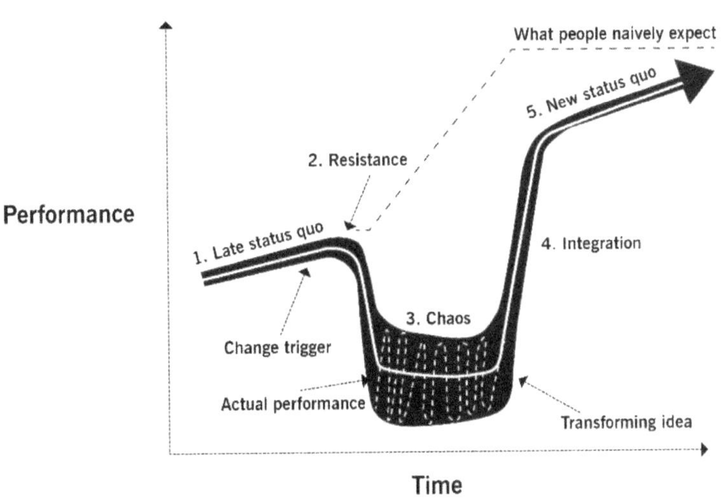

Figure 33: Satir change model[44]

Organisations that give up too soon will return to the status quo. Organisations that continue will be more likely to achieve their goals, and will also build capabilities that will benefit them for future change initiatives.

Satir can be combined with Kotter's eight-step process to help leaders deliver transformational change. Kotter's eight steps are:

---

[44] *ITIL® 4: Digital and IT Strategy*, Figure 6.1. ITIL® is a registered trade mark of the PeopleCert group. Used under licence from PeopleCert. All rights reserved.

- Create a sense of urgency;
- Build a guiding coalition;
- Form a strategic vision and initiatives;
- Enlist a volunteer army;
- Enable action by removing barriers;
- Generate quick wins;
- Sustain momentum; and
- Institute change.

You will notice how these steps reflect some of the advice in earlier chapters.

Leaders can also use the ADKAR model to help people embrace change; ADKAR focuses on awareness, desire, knowledge, ability and reinforcement.

Finally, the 7-S model (Peters and Waterman, 2004) can be used to express the elements that need to be managed and coordinated during transformation:

- Shared values, principles and beliefs
- Strategy
- Structure
- System
- Style
- Staff
- Skills

Managing strategic initiatives

Strategic initiatives are projects or programmes to be managed, so it makes sense to manage them like any other project or programme. However, there are some differences to be aware of:

- Projects or programmes may be linked to one or more strategies. Strategic changes will lead to project/programme changes, so the chosen project management approach needs to be agile.
- The project will need to be measured by whether it benefitted the organisation and supported its vision, not just the more traditional cost/quality/time metrics.
- Status and progress will need to be reported directly to the strategy owners.

Strategic initiatives can be implemented as a large-scale transformation or using a more incremental approach. The table below provides more explanation of the two approaches.

Table 33: Different transformation approaches

Large-scale transformation	The benefit of this approach is that it moves the whole organisation to the desired future state at once; perhaps in reaction to a threat or an opportunity. However, the challenge is that it can be difficult and disruptive to implement. It cannot succeed without commitment, alignment and focus between teams. This type of approach requires: • Coordination between leaders;

	• Coordination between teams and projects; • Integrated metrics and reporting; • Challenge to any instances of bureaucracy; and • All aspects of the organisation to be addressed; paced to areas that are most difficult or take longest to change.
Incremental transformation	This approach breaks the transformation down into smaller sections. It may start with a pilot, perhaps for a team, division, department or value stream. The learnings from the pilot can be applied to the next project, and pilot teams can coach and mentor the teams in the next stage. For this to be effective, individual stages and the overall transformation need to be measured and managed. The long-term focus must be maintained, while demonstrating patience and realistic expectations for how long change will take.

Mergers and acquisitions

Mergers and acquisitions also need to be considered for strategic coordination and implementation. Organisations can use mergers and acquisitions to acquire new technologies, market spaces or digital capabilities. A successful merger or acquisition relies on these critical success factors:

- Agree the new joint vision.
- Align the strategies of each organisation.
- Map and align practices.
- Culture will evolve to something between both organisation's starting points.
- Facilitate cultural change through metrics and communication aligned to the new joint vision and strategy.

Individual changes

A 'grassroots' strategy is one that starts in an individual area of an organisation and then spreads. These can be highly effective, but can sometimes be distracting and divert an organisation away from its overall vision. Grassroots initiatives should be subject to good governance, allowing leaders to balance the potential for innovation with maintaining the overall strategic direction. Tools and techniques like the Lean Change Management canvas (2014) can be used to help test ideas and individual changes.

Parallel operating models

During a digital transformation initiative, an organisation must still deliver and support existing products and services. Many digital transformations fail, perhaps because organisations must continue to deliver the 'norm' while progressing through transformation efforts. The goals of 'old' and 'new' may conflict, which can create a temporary chaotic state.

Parallel operating models (POMs) can allow an organisation to implement its digital strategy while maintaining steady state operations. They allow, in effect, two operating models to run at the same time. We're going to review four different types of POM:

- Cannibalism
- Erosion
- Concurrence
- Synergism

Cannibalism

This type of POM is focused on the rapid destruction of the existing business model and complete replacement with a new digital business model. This POM aims to reduce the time spent in parallel operation, making it the most aggressive of the POMs. It may be adopted in reaction to a threat, or be driven by an overcrowded market space with new competitors.

Some organisations will use this POM once (for example, an organisation that is making a move from a printed magazine to an online publication). Others carry out ongoing proactive cannibalism, for example Netflix moving from DVD rentals to consumer provider, to streaming video, to content creator (and perhaps advertising platform in the future?). There are also examples of continuous cannibalism, for example Apple replacing the Mac with the iPad, the iPod with the iPhone.

Erosion

Erosion is a gentler form of cannibalism. It aims to use the revenues of an existing and still profitable business model to fund a new digital business model, eventually allowing the old business model to decay and be retired. Erosion is characterised by three basic conditions:

- *"The existing business model does not benefit from the new digital business model*
- *The new digital business model needs the existing business model for a time (for its revenues)*
- *The new digital business model tends to destroy the old business model over time"*

Concurrence

Concurrence is an approach where the new digital business model neither helps nor harms the existing business model. It works best when an organisation is trying to increase or gain market share, or when consumers are difficult to reach via existing channels. For example, a farmer selling produce at a weekly farmers market may offer delivery boxes to people living outside the area. These consumers will probably never visit the market, so there is no overlap between the consumer groups.

Synergism

Synergism POMs are based on the idea that two models, when combined, can produce a different or better result than they can when working individually. In other words, the whole is greater than the sum of the parts.

This approach works best when there are existing adjacent or complementary sales channels, with no competition between channels and customers who prefer omnichannel access. This is the most mature/advanced POM, delivering real benefits but also challenging to execute.

An example could be an organisation selling specialist running shoes. They will have their in-store fitting service and guarantee, but also need to have an online presence, links to review sites and athletics groups, allowing them to access their potential customers wherever they are. Allowing a customer to search for shoes online, read reviews but then come into store for a fitting ensures they capture their market.

Ineffective models

The worst POM is having no POM at all. Organisations that don't have a POM are lucky if they manage to stay in business. Some organisations will adopt the wrong type of POM for their objectives, and others will adopt a POM approach accidentally when reacting to a change. The characteristics of ineffective models include:

- *"Being constructed without an outcomes-based view*
- *Not accounting for alternative models or realistic scenarios*
- *Being constructed as a response to extreme risk attitudes*
- *Being based on a misunderstanding of the current business model*
- *Not being sufficiently flexible, and not accounting for the potential need for repositioning"*

Transition pace

The best type of POM and the best speed for a transition will vary from organisation to organisation. These four areas need to be considered when setting the desired transition pace:

- Consumer demand – what do your consumers want?
- Organisational capabilities and culture.
- Maturity of any supporting digital technologies.
- Threats from competitors and emerging technologies.

Once an organisation completes a transition, it will have better capabilities to manage change. Change becomes the norm and there will be less fear of failure. This allows an organisation to adopt a continual improvement approach, seeking new digital models that will help them achieve their goals.

Assessing success

Strategy management will continually measure, review and update the organisation's overall direction as its environment changes. This process is supported by strategic measurement and reporting.

The old expression that 'we can't manage what we can't measure' doesn't necessarily apply in digital organisations. Management can be achieved through leadership, communication or design intuition. However, measurement is still important and can help:

- Influence behaviour
- Justify change
- Validate decisions
- Intervene when required

Measurement, metrics and indicators definitions

The three most common measurement categories are:

- Performance

- Maturity
- Compliance

Metrics are used to support measurement. The main types of metric are as follows:

- **Effectiveness:** measures whether an activity fulfils its purpose and achieves its objectives.
- **Efficiency:** measures how resources are used to perform activities or manage products and services.
- **Productivity:** shows the throughput of a resource or system; how much work is performed and the outputs.
- **Conformance:** whether an object meets agreed rules and requirements.

The four main types of metrics are effectiveness, efficiency, productivity and conformance. Suggest some examples for the Banksbest My Way project and some of its component services.

Organisations also need to balance lagging and leading metrics:

- **Lagging metrics:** report what has been achieved, cannot be influenced and are relatively easy to measure.
- **Leading metrics:** help predict what is likely to happen; more difficult to measure but can be influenced.

And finally, we should consider outside-in and inside-out metrics:

- **Outside-in:** give a customers' view of the organisation's services, and can be used to drive priorities and actions to meet customer needs.
- **Inside-out:** give an internal organisational view of services. However, these can be a constraint if they force customers to align with how the organisation works rather than changing the organisation to focus on customer needs.

The table below shows some more key definitions.

Table 34: Measurement definitions

Term	Definition
Metric	*"Measurement or calculation that is monitored or reported for management and improvement"*
Indicator	*"Metric that is used to assess and manage something"*
Key performance indicator	*"Important metric that is used to evaluate the success in meeting an objective"*
Performance	*"Measure of what is achieved or delivered by a system, person, team, practice, or service"*

Metrics add value when they support decision making by indicating something important or useful about the thing they are measuring. The most important metrics become key performance indicators (KPIs). A metric is a KPI when it provides crucial information about an object and its state. It must have an agreed target value and a tolerance range, for example the number of users a website has capacity for. The values can be tracked over time to create trends that can be analysed.

Many organisations increase the amount of things they report on each year. Think about the metrics and KPIs that are part of your role, or a previous role.

Are the KPIs really key? Are you measuring anything that you don't need to? Is there anything that you should be measuring that you don't?

To use metrics as KPIs, you need to:

- Identify what the 'key' metrics are;
- Define the target values and trends you need to measure; and
- Define the associated tolerances.

Figure 34 shows how measurements should be aligned and should cascade between different levels. If each level of measurement is operating in a silo, the organisation will not have a holistic view. Different audiences need to see different information; a service manager may need, for example, more operational detail than a service owner who is interested in how the service is performing overall.

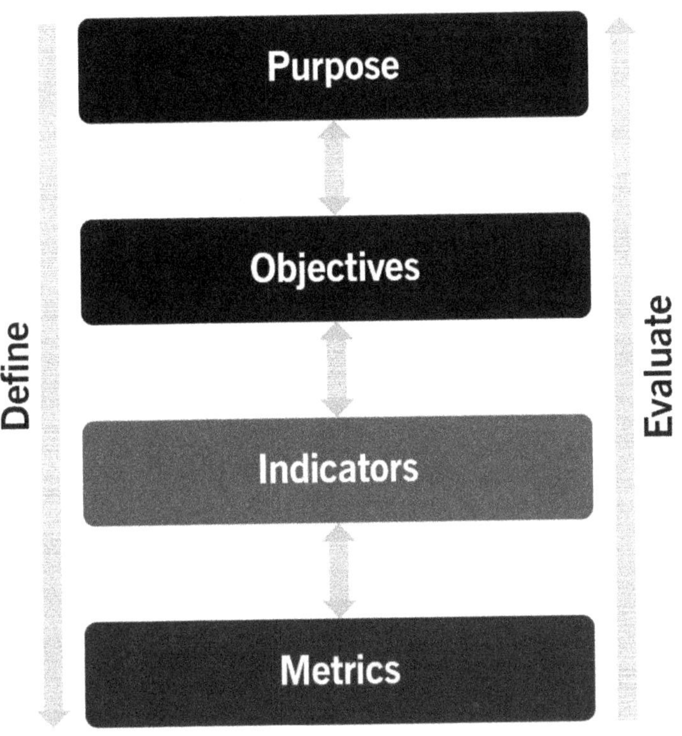

Figure 34: Planning and evaluation model[45]

The measurement and reporting practice outlines the steps for designing a measurement system. They are:

---

[45] *ITIL® 4: Digital and IT Strategy*, Figure 7.2. ITIL® is a registered trade mark of the PeopleCert group. Used under licence from PeopleCert.

- Define objectives;
- Identify the relevant success factors;
- Select the metrics and measurement tools or systems;
- Create the KPIs; and
- Aggregate measurement data.

The table below shows some examples of metrics.

Table 35: Examples of objectives, indicators, and metrics at different levels of management[46]

Focus	***Purpose***	***Objectives***	***Indicators***	***Metrics***
Strategy	*The purpose of the organization defining the strategy*	*Strategic objectives, such as ability to operate in a particular market or grow a particular line of business*	*Outcome-based*	*Organizational achievements (such as revenue growth level attained, market share), benchmark results*
Strategic initiative	*To implement an aspect of the organization's strategy (e.g. build a new product, create a new customer engagement model)*	*Project objectives, such as time to complete, budget, specifications*	*Achievement-based*	*Milestones met, money spent, resource utilization, specifications complied with*

[46] *ITIL® 4: Digital and IT Strategy*, Table 7.1. ITIL® is a registered trade mark of the PeopleCert group. Used under licence from PeopleCert. All rights reserved.

Function/ department or team operations	*To use the resources, tools, processes, etc. defined by the organization to perform the roles assigned to them (e.g. manufacture products, sell products)*	*Operational objectives, such as work rates, production levels, output quality*	*Performance -based*	*Revenue generated, expenses, productivity (quantity, quality, and timing), audits*
Order/service request /incident/change/etc.	*To identify, process, and complete items of work assigned to a function, team etc.*	*Process objectives, such as ticket duration, quantity, frequency, maximum cost*	*Occurrence-based*	*Number completed, time to complete, cost per ticket, revenue per ticket, occurrence patterns*

Objectives and key results (OKRs)

An OKR is *"a framework for defining and tracking objectives and their outcomes"*. Using OKRs helps an organisation focus on defining strategic objectives and the associated outcomes necessary to achieve them. Achieving an objective must provide value for the organisation.

Objectives are 'what' descriptors. They will:

- Express goals and intents;
- Be aggressive, yet realistic; and
- Be tangible, objective and unambiguous so that it's obvious an objective has been achieved.

Key results are 'how'. They will:

- Express measurable milestones that, if achieved, will advance the objective(s);
- Describe outcomes, not activities; and
- Include evidence of completion.

Figure 35 shows how OKRs can be used to bridge the gap between strategy and execution. Many digital organisations have adopted OKRs. The Google OKR playbook is a valuable resource if you wish to learn more.

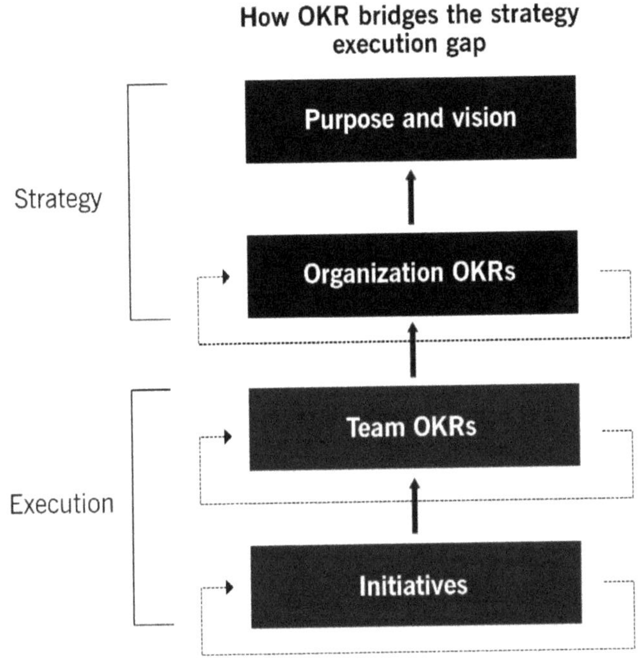

Figure 35: How OKRs bridge strategy and execution (adapted with permission from Perdoo, 2020)[47]

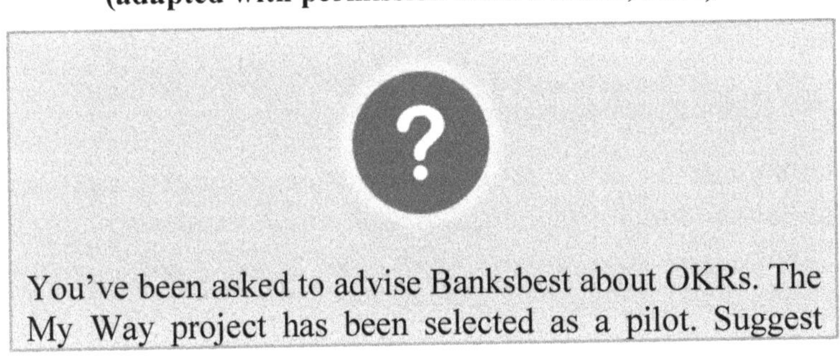

You've been asked to advise Banksbest about OKRs. The My Way project has been selected as a pilot. Suggest

[47] *ITIL® 4: Digital and IT Strategy*, Figure 7.3. Adapted from Perdoo (2020), The ultimate guide to OKR, *https://www.perdoo.com/the-ultimate-okr-guide/*. ITIL® is a registered trade mark of the PeopleCert group. Used under licence from PeopleCert. All rights reserved.

examples of OKRs that could be used to measure My Way.

Measuring a strategy

Principles for measuring a strategy include the following:

- Match the measurement frequency to organisational volatility; more stable organisations can review less frequently than those undergoing high levels of change.
- Adjust and evolve the existing strategy; don't start a new strategy each time unless there has been a complete failure.
- Align budgeting policies with the strategy cycle, aligning financial reporting with strategic initiatives.
- Align operational reports and strategic reports; this will make it easier to measure strategic performance.

There are three main reasons to measure a strategy:

- **Progress:** is it being implemented as planned?
- **Performance:** is it achieving objectives?
- **Relevance:** does it need to change?

Organisations also need to measure whether strategic initiatives are proceeding on time, to specification and to budget. If there is any deviation, leaders will need to decide on the action to take. They could:

- Allocate additional funding to an initiative;
- Revise the timelines of the strategy;
- Alert key stakeholders of delays (or acceleration) to the delivery of a particular outcome;

- Decide on whether to continue with the initiative or switch to an alternative; and
- Adjust the strategy as appropriate.

Another question that leaders will need to answer is whether the strategic initiatives and the overall strategy are meeting their objectives. Initiatives may be on time and on budget, but the strategy overall is no longer fully fit for purpose. If action needs to be taken here, leaders can:

- Change the strategy to respond to a particular event;
- Move to an alternative scenario;
- Allocate additional resources to one part of the organisation; or
- Withdraw from an opportunity or a market – cancelling that part of the strategy.

Any changes that are made will need to be communicated to all affected stakeholders (remember that this could include consumers).

Changes to an organisation's internal and external environment can mean strategic initiatives are no longer relevant (it may be doing things right, but not doing the right things). Regular reviews will allow leaders to assess the ongoing relevance of its strategy. Changes to the internal and external environment can be caused by external factors, but may even be a result of the strategy itself. For example, Banksbest may find that its new focus on digital initiatives means it is losing customers in an older age group who are not used to banking online. If a strategy isn't relevant, it is no longer viable.

Instrumenting strategy

This section of the ITIL® 4: Digital and IT Strategy publication draws on work from Isaychenko and Demin (2020).

Information and data are typically used for reports, but they can also be used for:

- Quality management
- Audits
- Continual improvement
- Service validation

Metrics should be relevant to the recipient and presented in a way that's easy to use and understand.

Reports contain measurements and outputs; for example, comparisons between actual and target values (to highlight deviations), actual and previous performance (trends), different indicators (to evaluate correlations, identify bottlenecks). These reports may be operational or analytical. They can explain why something is happening and recommend actions.

Operational reports/dashboards

Operational reports identify deviations from plans and/or objectives as they happen, which allows for rapid corrective action when needed. They are often automated, with little human interaction. They may have a high reporting frequency, providing regular up-to-date or real-time information to support decisions.

Dashboards are a type of operational report. They will:

- Present the most important indicators; and

- Provide information on a single screen.

Many organisations are moving to strategy dashboards (moving away from long, static documents) to provide real-time information and links to supporting data. This allows a better understanding of how a strategy is performing.

Analytical reports

Analytical reports can identify hidden issues, explain why things are happening and highlight improvement opportunities. Operational reports often present facts; analytical reports provide more detail about why things are happening and what might be done.

This type of report may not be fully automated, when human input is needed to interpret the data. They are typically less frequent and support longer-term decision making. They may contain sensitive information requiring approval for wider release.

The table below shows some of the differences between operational and analytical reports.

Table 36: Operational report vs. analytical report[48]

Property	*Operational report*	*Analytical report*
Purpose	*To deliver information to evaluate the current state, to*	*To deliver analytical evaluation of the managed object, to identify hidden issues*

[48] *ITIL® 4: Digital and IT Strategy*, Table 7.2. ITIL® is a registered trade mark of the PeopleCert group. Used under licence from PeopleCert.

	identify bottlenecks, and to support operational decisions	*and their causes, and to suggest improvement options*
Activity to produce	*Ongoing measurements of resources and operations*	*Targeted analytical research*
Content	• *Measurement results* • *Comparisons with the target and historic values* • *Matching different indicator values to identify correlations and bottlenecks*	*Content is driven by the research goal and analysis method; a sample table of contents can be as follows:* • *a structure of goals related to the management object, and its current state description* • *industry benchmarking* • *identified issues and their causes* • *conclusions and recommendations*
Production technology	*Automated, with minimal human labor*	*Manually created by a qualified analyst; such a report requires both data collection and human involvement in the form of interviews, workshops, and brainstorming*

Production time	*From several seconds to several hours*	*From several days to several months*
Decision horizon	*Not exceeding a quarter; normally within a month*	*From a quarter to several years*
Authorization	*Not required*	*Sometimes required*

Strategy review

The purpose of a strategy review is to ensure the ongoing relevance and effectiveness of a strategy. Every strategic cycle should include a review step to ensure that initiatives are being fulfilled within the defined and agreed scope.

The review should examine the impact of the actions taken and metrics used in the previous cycle, to assess both intended and unintended consequences. Metrics can drive bad behaviour, so it's important to identify this and correct where necessary.

Here's a quick example of metrics driving bad behaviour. Many years ago, I worked with a helpdesk that was given a new, aggressive target for 'time to answer'. The metric was intended to motivate the staff to finish calls quickly and pick up quickly when queues were building. Instead, in quiet periods the staff just called each other. They called, picked up quickly and hung up, over-achieving on their new target. We can't always see what behaviour a metric will drive, so we need to analyse it over time. We also need to create a balanced set of metrics that provide a holistic focus; in this case, for example, time to answer could be supplemented by number of tickets reopened, customer satisfaction, etc.

Data is useful but requires insight to be valuable. Insight describes the ability to gain an accurate and deep understanding of a situation. Insight is a 'human' characteristic implying emotion, experience and feelings. At present, it can't be produced by artificial intelligence or automation.

Techniques like ALOE (ask, listen, observe, empathise) can be used to support an organisation's performance and evolution, creating emotional, social and system intelligence.

Practice: Measurement and reporting

Purpose

The purpose of the measurement and reporting practice is to *"support good decision-making and continual improvement by decreasing the levels of uncertainty"*.

The practice uses data collected from:

- Products and services;
- Practices and value chain activities;
- Teams and individuals;
- Suppliers and partners; and
- The organisation as a whole.

The practice uses critical success factors (CSFs) for each objective and then KPIs to assess each CSF. This provides granularity and transparency.

Measures need to be linked to organisational objectives, such as customer and market relevant, and operational excellence.

Practice success factors

There are three PSFs defined for the measurement and reporting practice:

- Ensure measurements are driven by objectives
- Ensure the quality and availability of measurement data
- Ensure there is effective reporting to support decision-making

Table 37: Measurement and reporting PSFs

PSF: Ensure measurements are driven by objectives
Measurements only have value if they are aligned with organisational objectives. There are five steps to create a measurement and evaluation system: 1. Define the objectives: what will the system be used for? What is most important? Look, for example, at effectiveness, conformance, efficiency and productivity measures. 2. Identify success factors. 3. Select metrics and measurement tools; can we measure what we need to? 4. Form a system of KPIs. 5. Aggregate measurement data.

The measurements can then be expressed in 'zones' showing red/amber/green status.
PSF: Ensure the quality and availability of measurement data
Incomplete, inconsistent or poor-quality data leads to poor decision making. High-quality data will be: • Intrinsically good (accurate, objective, believable, etc.); • Contextually appropriate (complete, relevant, timely, etc.); • Clearly represented (understandable, consistent, interpretable, etc.); and • Accessible (available as and when agreed). All practices that keep records can help ensure quality data, for example the service desk, and monitoring and event management. Practices that help ensure the availability of information include availability management and information security management.
PSF: Ensure there is effective reporting to support decision-making
To develop an effective report, we need to understand: • Who is the report consumer? • What is the purpose of the report? What decisions should it support? • Who will generate and work with the report? • How will the report be used?

- What data should the report contain?
- How will the report data be structured and displayed?

Data structures include grouped KPIs (in logical blocks), aggregated KPIs, a structure that identifies bottlenecks, and different visualisation options (tables, charts, etc.).

Digital transformation activities

The activities linked to any digital transformation will be dictated by its scope and objectives. In this section, we will look at two scenarios and some of the typical digital transformation activities. You can use these as the basis for transformations that you work on, but you will need to adapt them each time to suit the individual circumstances. The ITIL® 4 project management practice guide also has further supporting information.

Scenario 1: Build capabilities to become a digital organisation

Figure 36 summarises this approach.[49]

[49] *ITIL® 4: Digital and IT Strategy*, Figure 6.3. ITIL® is a registered trade mark of the PeopleCert group. Used under licence from PeopleCert. All rights reserved.

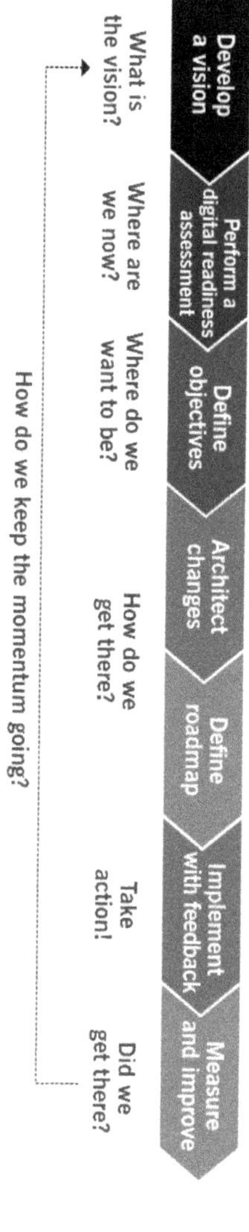

Figure 36: Typical steps in a digital transformation programme

In this scenario (often called a 'digital strategy'), an organisation will create a digital task force to define and implement a transformation programme. This will include senior leaders, subject matter experts and customer experience representatives. This scenario will usually result in a series of initiatives, gradually building the capabilities that the organisation needs.

For this scenario to be effective, the organisation will need:

- Good governance;
- Leadership (from more than just a single individual); and
- Collaboration.

Scenario 2: Perform a single digital transformation initiative

This approach often occurs when an organisation already has a level of digital maturity. A stakeholder or group of stakeholders will see an opportunity to use digital technology to do something better, faster or cheaper.

This is a more tactical or operational approach, but can still deliver organisational impact as the number of individual projects or initiatives grows. Careful management is required to ensure that:

- There is no duplication or overlap;
- Each initiative has a defined and accepted business case;
- The initiatives are consistent with the organisation's overall strategy; and
- The initiatives are compliant with strategic policies, architectural guidelines, etc.

In this scenario, it's important to manage the initiatives in the same way as any other project or programme. The organisation also needs to recognise that these types of initiative can have wider consequences than a typical project or programme, particularly where they affect ways of working. The organisation will need to carry out an additional assessment of the initiative's impact on the overall strategy, look for any lessons learned that have a broader application, and provide reports to strategic leaders.

CHAPTER 9: EXAM PREPARATION

The ITIL® 4: Digital and IT Strategy exam may be different to other ITIL® 4 exams that you've taken. In addition to the multiple-choice exam, there are four practical assignments that you need to complete and submit to your training organisation. In this chapter, you'll find guidance for both the practical assignments and the multiple-choice exam.

Practical assignment guidance

Your training organisation will give you guidance on how and when to submit your practical assignment answers. These are usually sent in as MS Word or PDF documents. I recommend keeping copies of your practical assignment answers after submission.

You must be able to apply the ITIL® 4 guiding principles to the assignments, regardless of which organisation you choose. Here are some tips to help you complete your assignments successfully:

- Read the question carefully and understand what is being asked. You are not required to write a book – concise answers that clearly demonstrate your understanding are most appreciated and are all that is required.
- Use any forms provided – they will help you answer concisely.
- Choose only one organisation from the case study and answer based on that organisation throughout all assignments. Do NOT forget the risk report.

- If you make any assumptions, call out the assumption(s) clearly. Repeat your assumptions if they carry over to other assignments.
- When you are asked to pick a strategy, pick ONE and perhaps add a sentence to defend your choice; don't create an answer for all choices.
- Be sure to fully answer the question – there are some questions with multiple parts. If you are asked for three or five examples, provide that number – you don't get bonus points for providing more and you lose points for less.
- Be sure to use ITIL® 4: Digital and IT Strategy guidance where possible, but common sense that is pragmatic and logical will work. You will not receive full credit for the answer without incorporating this guidance.
- Remember that your answers, collectively across all four assignments, are completing a story of sorts. Ensure what you suggest flows and is sensible.
- When answering the guiding principle questions, you may be asked to create a list, but it's also important to provide a short reason the guiding principle has been chosen and how it is applied (e.g. what benefit does it provide? What is its impact on the scenario?).
- Choose two to four of the most relevant guiding principles – you are not expected to list/explain all guiding principles for each question.

In summary: clear and concise answers will be most appreciated by your instructor – answer the question, no more, no less!

ITIL® 4: Digital and IT Strategy multiple-choice exam

Here are the key facts about the ITIL® 4: Digital and IT Strategy multiple-choice exam. This may also be slightly different to other ITIL exams you've taken.

- The exam is 60 minutes long. Extra time is allowable if English is not your native language and a translated paper isn't available.
- The exam is closed book – it's just you and your knowledge.
- It has 30 multiple-choice questions, and you must get 21 correct, or 70%, to pass.
- There is no negative marking (so you don't lose a mark if you get a question wrong).

Your training provider for ITIL® 4: Digital and IT Strategy will provide you with access to at least one sample exam. When you're ready to attempt the sample paper, try to reproduce, as far as possible, the conditions of the real exam.

Set aside 60 minutes to complete the paper and make sure there are no distractions: don't make a coffee; don't raid the refrigerator; don't check your emails or social media; and switch off your phone.

If you don't focus exclusively on the sample exam questions, you will not have a good indication of your possible performance in the live exam. Your sample exam may highlight areas for further study before you take your final exam.

Here are some good practices for taking multiple-choice exams:

Manage your time: If you're stuck on a question, mark it and go back to it later. It's easy to spend too long staring at one question, but there may be easier marks to be picked up further on in the paper.

Have a technique: I like to go through a paper and complete all the questions I feel confident about first. That allows me to see how many of the more challenging ones I need to get right to pass.

Trust your instinct: One of the most common bits of exam feedback is candidates who wish they had not changed their answer at the last minute. It's fine to check over what you've done, but be very wary about making changes in those last few seconds.

Use the process of elimination: Each question has four possible answers. If you can discount one or two, you've dramatically increased your odds of picking the right answer.

Don't panic!: If your mind goes blank, move to another question – you can do this with online and paper exams. Your subconscious mind will work away even when you're answering a different question.

Read the question carefully: If you're not careful, you will answer the question you **think** you see, not the one that's actually there.

And that's all from me! I hope you've enjoyed the book. The extra content I've provided along the way will help you start using ITIL® 4: Digital and IT Strategy concepts in your own role. You can find me on LinkedIn and Twitter – I'd love to hear if you've enjoyed the book and how your studies and your exam help you in your career.

APPENDIX A: BANKSBEST CASE STUDY

Company overview

Banksbest was originally HW Banking. It was founded in 1953 in the UK and has branches in most major UK cities. It focuses mainly on business clients, but it also has a mortgage department that offers residential mortgages to aspiring homeowners and buy-to-let mortgages to landlords.

The Banksbest board of directors initiated a digital transformation programme in 2017. At the same time, a new CEO and a new CIO were recruited. A Chief Digital Officer (CDO) role has also been established. As part of the digital transformation programme, the bank rebranded from HW Banking to Banksbest, which was seen as a more customer-focused brand.

Banksbest has defined these strategic goals:

- To be the tenth largest provider of business banking services in the UK (growing its customer base by approximately 25%).
- To grow its residential mortgage business by 50%.
- To build a reputation as a 'digital first' banking provider.

There is some conflict during board meetings, as the CFO is not fully convinced about the value of the CDO role and the digital transformation programme. She would prefer to focus on cost management.

The head office and data centre for Banksbest are in Manchester. The customer service centre is in Reading. There is also an agreement with a business process outsourcing company in Bulgaria, Employeez on Demand, that provides additional customer service resources during peak times. The customer service centre operates 7 days a week, between 8:00 am and 6:00 pm, and support is also available via the bank's website on a 24x7 basis.

Banksbest's 50 branches are open Monday to Saturday, between 9:00 am and 5:00 pm.

Banksbest has a good reputation in a competitive field. However, the rebrand has confused some customers, and the digital transformation programme has not delivered many measurable results yet. Banksbest needs to improve its online services and embed its new brand to grow.

Company structure

Banksbest employs 700 staff. 400 of these work in the bank's branches, 100 in the call centre, and 200 in head office and support functions. Additional staff are supplied by Employeez on Demand during peak times.

Banksbest is split into divisions:

- **Central Operations** – provides support services for all departments. Operations includes HR, Finance, Marketing and IT. The IT department has 50 staff.
- **Customer Services** – this department includes the staff who work in and manage the customer service centre, as well as technical specialists who work on the systems used in the customer service centre.
- **Branches** – this department is responsible for the branches providing face-to-face banking services. The branches are expensive to maintain but offer a face-to-face service that some Banksbest customers value.

The digital transformation programme is being run by a digital team that operates outside the existing divisions.

Future plans

To achieve its goals, Banksbest and the digital transformation programme team are working on different initiatives. These include the flagship 'My Way' project, which will allow business banking customers to access services however suits them best. Commissioned by the CDO and led by a product owner, My Way will allow business banking customers to use a range of devices to manage their accounts and move seamlessly between branch-based and online transactions. The current plans include:

- Testing biometrics including fingerprint and voice login to support My Way;
- My Deposit My Way, allowing cheques to be paid in using the camera on a mobile phone; and
- Monitoring of customer feedback, levels of demand, and which products are most popular.

After three months, the product owner will report back to the CDO. At this point, the project will either be allocated additional funding, will pivot, or will be closed down. My Way is being measured on both governance and compliance and customer satisfaction outcomes.

IT services

All the IT services are run from head office and the Manchester data centre. Since the digital transformation programme started, more services are Cloud hosted by external providers. The main IT services are as follows:

Bizbank – the banking system used in the branches and customer service centre. This system contains customer account information and history, including current and savings accounts. Bizbank is hosted in the Manchester data centre, but there are plans to move it to a Cloud hosting service to improve its resilience. Bizbank incidents sometimes take a long time to resolve because the original developers have left, and documentation is poor.

Mortbank – the mortgage system used in branches and the customer service centre. As well as tracking existing mortgages, Mortbank has a credit-checking facility that supports mortgage approvals. Mortbank was developed by MortSys, which provides ongoing support and maintenance. MortSys is a small organisation and doesn't always respond within its agreed target times.

Mibank – an online self-service portal being developed as part of the My Way project. Mibank allows customers to check their accounts, move money between accounts, pay bills and receive cheques. The functionality of Mibank will expand as the My Way project progresses.

Banksec – an identity-checking utility that is used by Bizbank, Mortbank and Mibank. Banksec uses two-factor authentication, and biometric capabilities are in development.

IT department

The IT department includes 50 staff split into 4 departments, under the CIO:

- Strategic Planning and Business Relationship Management.
- Service Management.

- Development.
- Operations (including Service Desk).

IT has a good reputation generally, but business staff see the IT department as responsible for day-to-day operations and fixing things. The IT department's development role is less well understood. There is also some friction between the digital transformation programme staff and IT staff.

IT service management

Service management does not have a high profile in Banksbest.

The CIO holds a position at board level, and likes to be seen as dynamic and responsive, rather than process driven and bureaucratic. However, some recent service outages have led to interest in service management best practices, as well as assessment of other ways of working including DevOps, Agile and Lean.

There are some culture issues in the IT department, including an 'us and them' attitude that means developers and operations staff don't always work well together.

Sample employee biographies

Lucy Jones	Lucy joined Banksbest as a graduate trainee five years ago. As part of her training, she spent six months in each of the major departments: Central Operations, Branches and Customer Services. During her time in Central Operations, she spent two months in Finance, two months in HR and two months in IT, including working on the Service Desk.

	Following completion of her graduate trainee programme, Lucy was offered a job in HR, and worked there for three years. She was then offered a newly created role of Product Owner and is now responsible for the 'My Way' project. Lucy has a good understanding of the Banksbest business units and the IT services that support them.

Doug Range	Doug has worked for Banksbest for 20 years since it was HW Banking. He started work as counter staff in one of the branches and worked his way up to branch manager. His branch was chosen to be one of the pilot locations for the rollout of Bizbank, some years ago, and for two years he acted as a super-user for this system, logging the queries he handled onto the service desk system. He has recently been promoted to a head office role, including training the customer service centre staff. Doug is working with Lucy on the My Way project, helping to provide customer intelligence, and ensuring the customer service centre staff are kept up to date.

FURTHER READING

IT Governance Publishing (ITGP) is the world's leading publisher for governance and compliance. Our industry-leading pocket guides, books and training resources are written by real-world practitioners and thought leaders. They are used globally by audiences of all levels, from students to C-suite executives.

Our high-quality publications cover all IT governance, risk and compliance frameworks and are available in a range of formats. This ensures our customers can access the information they need in the way they need it.

Our other ITIL publications include:

- *ITIL® 4 Direct, Plan and Improve (DPI) – Your companion to the ITIL 4 Managing Professional DPI certification* by Claire Agutter, *https://www.itgovernance.co.uk/shop/product/itil-4-direct-plan-and-improve-dpi*
- *ITIL® 4 Create, Deliver and Support (CDS) – Your companion to the ITIL 4 Managing Professional CDS certification* by Claire Agutter, *https://www.itgovernance.co.uk/shop/product/itil-4-create-deliver-and-support-cds-your-companion-to-the-itil-4-managing-professional-cds-certification*
- *ITIL® 4 Drive Stakeholder Value (DSV) – Your companion to the ITIL 4 Managing Professional DSV certification* by Claire Agutter, *https://www.itgovernance.co.uk/shop/product/itil-4-*

drive-stakeholder-value-dsv-your-companion-to-the-itil-4-managing-professional-dsv-certification

- *ITIL® 4 High-Velocity IT (HVIT) – Your companion to the ITIL 4 Managing Professional HVIT certification* by Claire Agutter, *https://www.itgovernance.co.uk/shop/product/itil-4-high-velocity-it-hvit-your-companion-to-the-itil-4-managing-professional-hvit-certification*

For more information on ITGP and branded publishing services, and to view our full list of publications, visit *www.itgovernancepublishing.co.uk*.

To receive regular updates from ITGP, including information on new publications in your area(s) of interest, sign up for our newsletter:

www.itgovernancepublishing.co.uk/topic/newsletter.

Branded publishing

Through our branded publishing service, you can customise ITGP publications with your company's branding.

Find out more at

www.itgovernancepublishing.co.uk/topic/branded-publishing-services.

Related services

ITGP is part of GRC International Group, which offers a comprehensive range of complementary products and services to help organisations meet their objectives.

For a full range of GCR International Group's resources, visit *www.itgovernance.co.uk/*.

Training services

The IT Governance training programme is built on our extensive practical experience designing and implementing management systems based on ISO standards, best practice and regulations.

Our courses help attendees develop practical skills and comply with contractual and regulatory requirements. They also support career development via recognised qualifications.

Learn more about our training courses and view the full course catalogue at *www.itgovernance.co.uk/training*.

Professional services and consultancy

We are a leading global consultancy of IT governance, risk management and compliance solutions. We advise businesses around the world on their most critical issues and present cost-saving and risk-reducing solutions based on international best practice and frameworks.

We offer a wide range of delivery methods to suit all budgets, timescales and preferred project approaches.

Find out how our consultancy services can help your organisation at *www.itgovernance.co.uk/consulting*.

Industry news

Want to stay up to date with the latest developments and resources in the IT governance and compliance market? Subscribe to our Weekly Round-up newsletter and we will send you mobile-friendly emails with fresh news and features about your preferred areas of interest, as well as unmissable offers and free resources to help you successfully start your projects. *www.itgovernance.co.uk/weekly-round-up*.

EU for product safety is Stephen Evans, The Mill Enterprise Hub, Stagreenan, Drogheda, Co. Louth, A92 CD3D, Ireland. (servicecentre@itgovernance.eu)

www.ingramcontent.com/pod-product-compliance
Lightning Source LLC
Chambersburg PA
CBHW041636050326
40690CB00026B/5240

* 9 7 8 1 7 8 7 7 8 4 2 6 0 *